Working with
Tablesaws

Working with Tablesaws

The Editors of
Fine Woodworking

The Taunton Press

The Taunton Press
Inspiration for hands-on living®

The Taunton Press, Inc., 63 South Main Street, PO Box 5506, Newtown, CT 06470-5506
e-mail: tp@taunton.com

Jacket/cover design: Susan Fazekas
Interior design and layout: Susan Fazekas
Front cover photographer: Mark Schofield, courtesy *Fine Woodworking,*
© The Taunton Press, Inc.
Back cover photographers: Anatole Burkin, courtesy *Fine Woodworking,* © The Taunton
Press, Inc. (top), Strother Purdy, courtesy *Fine Woodworking,* © The Taunton Press,
Inc. (bottom)

The New Best of Fine Woodworking® is a trademark of The Taunton Press, Inc.,
registered in the U.S. Patent and Trademark Office.

Library of Congress Cataloging-in-Publication Data

Working with tablesaws / the editors of Fine woodworking.
       p. cm. -- (The new best of fine woodworking)
    ISBN 1-56158-749-4
    1. Circular saws. 2. Woodworking tools. I. Fine woodworking II. Series.
    TT186.W6765 2005
    684'.083--dc22

                                    2004018019

Printed in the United States of America
10 9 8 7 6 5 4 3 2

The following manufacturers/names appearing in *Working with Tablesaws* are trademarks:
Biesemeyer®, Bridgewood®, CMT®, Craftsman®, Delrin®, Delta®, De-Sta-Co®,
DeWalt®, Formica®, Freud®, General®, Grizzly®, Jesada Tools®, Jet®, Oldham®,
Plexiglas®, Powermatic®, Sears®, Scotch®, Starrett®, Styrofoam®, Tenryu®, TopCote®,
Unifence®, Unisaw®, Vermont American®, Woodtek®, Woodworker's Supply^{SM}, X-Acto®

Working wood is inherently dangerous. Using hand or power tools improperly or ignoring
safety practices can lead to permanent injury or even death. Don't try to perform operations
you learn about here (or elsewhere) unless you're certain they are safe for you. If something
about an operation doesn't feel right, don't do it. Look for another way. We want you to enjoy the craft, so please keep safety foremost in your mind whenever you're in the shop.

Acknowledgments

Special thanks to the authors, editors,
art directors, copy editors, and other
staff members of *Fine Woodworking* who
contributed to the development of the
articles in this book.

Contents

Introduction

My first major machine-tool purchase was a garage-sale tablesaw. The tool was all cast iron and sheet metal. There was very little rust to be found, suggesting a well-cared-for history, and it appeared to include all of the necessary parts. When I hit the power switch, the motor came to life with a powerful, satisfying hum. But try as I might, I was unable to rip a board with parallel edges or crosscut stock squarely.

My frustration increased, as the owner's manual was not much help. It told me how to assemble the various parts and suggested I should not operate the tool while on drugs or while standing in a puddle of water. Good advice for someone, I imagine. As I went over the machine, I realized that my ignorance was not limited to technique: This saw was in need of a tune-up.

I wish I had this book then. Over the years, *Fine Woodworking* magazine has published a number of articles on how to use machines safely and efficiently and what to do when they get out of tune. This book is a collection of those articles, including such topics as how to straighten warped lumber on a jointer, choose the best bandsaw blade

for a particular job, or set the blade of a tablesaw parallel to the miter-gauge slot.

Whether you are just starting out in woodworking and need instruction on the basics of how to use machines to get flat, square stock, or need more advanced tips on useful jigs for your machines, this book will take your woodworking to a higher level.

—Anatole Burkin, editor of
Fine Woodworking

Nine Midsize Tablesaws

BY ROLAND JOHNSON

When setting up a new workshop, the first big purchase for most people is a tablesaw. Priced and sized in between the large cabinet saws and small benchtop saws, a contractor-style saw is the logical choice for many woodworkers.

I surveyed several brands on the market and came away from the experience pleasantly surprised.

Seven of the machines I looked at are conventional contractor-style saws: Bridgewood® TSC-10CL, Delta® 36-426, General® 50-185M1, Grizzly® 1022ProZ, Jet® JWTS-10JF, Powermatic® 64A, and Woodtek® TSC-B. I also tested two hybrids—the DeWalt® DW746 and Jet JWSS-10LFR—which are designed to bridge the gap between contractor's and cabinet saws.

Overall Quality Has Improved

Not too many years ago, reasonably priced woodworking machinery often left a lot to be desired when it came to the quality of materials and machining. When it comes to contractor's saws, that appears to be a thing of the past.

I checked all of the tabletops for flatness. With the exception of the table on the Grizzly, all of the tables were nearly perfectly flat front to back, side to side, and diagonally. The miter slots were within 0.001 in. in width end to end; all of them were within 0.002 in. to 0.003 in. in width to each other; and all were within 0.004 in. of being perfectly parallel. The only flaws I found were that some of the table extensions tipped up

Testing Each Machine

Using a Starrett® straightedge and feeler gauges, Johnson checked the flatness of each table side to side (below), front to back, and diagonally. All but the Grizzly were notably flat. He used a Forrest testing disc to check runout (right), and checked whether the factory settings of the trunnions and motors were parallel to the miter-gauge slots in the tops. Johnson also ripped and crosscut 8/4 white oak and hard maple (see photo on facing page) as a real-world test of the machines under load.

at the outside edge, which could easily be remedied with a shim and a bit of tinkering.

Bevel and height adjusters worked well, and with all of these saws you can make adjustments in the gears that raise and lower the blade and change the angle setting. A lock knob in the crank handle of each saw secures the arbor's location, although the DeWalt would benefit from bigger crank handles.

I used a Forrest 10-in. testing disc—a sawblade blank that is accurate to within ± 0.001 in.—to test for runout at the rim of the blade. Runout on all of the saws was 0.004 in. or less: an acceptable tolerance.

Except for the Delta, which uses cast-aluminum pulleys, all of the saws use machined iron pulleys. A few of the saws could benefit from higher-quality belts, but most of them ran smoothly with little or no vibration. Only the Grizzly comes equipped with a link belt, which reduces vibration and makes the saw run more quietly.

In short, I was impressed with the overall fit and finish of these machines.

Good Fences Make Good Saws

Since the 1990s, tablesaw fences have improved. Bill Biesemeyer did the woodworking world a real favor when he designed his simple, effective, beam-style rip fence. The majority of the saws I looked at have a variation on the Biesemeyer-style fence, and the one thing they all have in common is a lack of measurable side deflection. The Powermatic and the Jet JWTS-10JF have identical fences, and the General and Grizzly have fences only

BRIDGEWOOD TSC-10CL

This was a good, solid saw at a low price. The only thing I didn't like about it was that the switch mount protruded too far out at the front of the saw.

Street price	$549
Motor	1½ hp/18 amp at 120 V
Blade tilt	Left
Maximum rip capacity	32 in.
Runout at rim of 10-in. testing disc	0.004 in.
Blade alignment	0.005 in. out of parallel
Dust collection	Tray in base of saw cabinet with 4-in.-diameter outlet

DELTA 36-426

The Delta was a well-made and appointed machine. The Delta Unifence was versatile, accurate, and easy to operate. However, the machine could use a better dust-collection system.

Street price	$849
Motor	1½ hp/12.8 amp at 120 V
Blade tilt	Right
Maximum rip capacity	32 in.
Runout at rim of 10-in. testing disc	0.003 in.
Blade alignment	0.002 in. out of parallel
Dust collection	Slanted, open tray between legs of stand

slightly different from those. The Woodtek and the Bridgewood saws also have fences identical to each other.

The General uses melamine for the faces of its fence, while the Grizzly, the Jets, and the Powermatic use UHMW (ultrahigh molecular weight) material for reduced friction. The Woodtek and the Bridgewood have a milled face on the aluminum extrusion that makes up the fence on each machine.

The General's fence is a closer copy of the original Biesemeyer fence in that the cam lever that locks it in place and the rail pad on which the fence glides are simpler than the others. Also, a rubber grommet on

GENERAL 50-185M1

The base offered storage areas for the miter gauge, rip fence, and wrenches—a nice touch. Ball detents in the miter-gauge bar ensured an accurate fit. With its left-tilting blade, powerful 2-hp motor, sturdy fence, and reasonable price, I considered this saw to be the best buy of the bunch.

Street price	$649
Motor	2 hp/15 amp at 120 V
Blade tilt	Left
Maximum rip capacity	30⅜ in.
Runout at rim of 10-in. testing disc	0.003 in.
Blade alignment	0.000 in. out of parallel
Dust collection	Tray in base of saw cabinet with 4-in.-diameter outlet

GRIZZLY 1022PROZ

The cabinet of the saw was welded slightly out of square, which made assembly difficult, and the top was the least flat of the bunch, with a 0.02-in.-deep dish across one diagonal. The Grizzly was the only saw that came with a link belt as standard issue, which made the machine run quieter.

Street price	$595
Motor	2 hp/16 amp at 120 V
Blade tilt	Right
Maximum rip capacity	25 in.
Runout at rim of 10-in. testing disc	0.003 in.
Blade alignment	0.004 in. out of parallel
Dust collection	Tray in base of saw cabinet with 4-in.-diameter outlet

the cam lever allows the lever to be locked in the up position, which makes it easier to remove the fence and to put it back on the rail.

Most of the fences can be adjusted to be brought parallel with the blade and square with the tabletop. The Delta Unifence® is a real gem to adjust: The parallel adjustments on the front of the fence are made with nuts that are the same size as the arbor nut, so the right wrench is always handy. Adjustments to square the face to the table are made with a screwdriver. The Unifence is by far the most user-friendly for setup, and there is no need for a rail at the back of the saw because the fence rides smoothly on a

Fence Should Be Easy to Read and Adjust

READABILITY

SOME FENCES ARE EASIER TO READ THAN OTHERS. The Align A Rip fence on the Woodtek and Bridgewood machines has a plastic magnifying lens that makes it easy to read the tape (below) The lens and the printed rule on the Jet SuperSaw (right) can be difficult to read from some angles.

ADJUSTABILITY

THREE SCREWS FOR THE DEWALT. The same three screws in the top of the DeWalt fence are used to set the fence square to the tabletop and parallel to the sawblade.

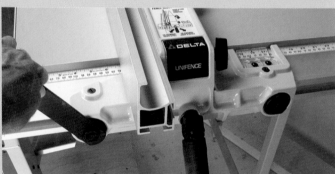

THE DELTA UNIFENCE IS UNIQUE. To adjust the Unifence square to the sawblade, you use the same wrench supplied with the saw for changing blades. The extruded-aluminum fence can be located in either a high or a low profile, to adjust for different ripping operations. Extruded flanges wrap around a flat metal bar that holds the fence tightly to either side of the main carriage to which it's attached.

nylon glide. The Unifence is also versatile because you can configure it for a low profile to perform different ripping operations.

The fence on the Jet SuperSaw (JWSS-10LFR) contains elements of the Biesemeyer style with a few twists, such as a rubber thumbwheel that operates on the front rail for finely tuning the fence setting. The rear support for the fence has a slot that fits over the edge of the back rail, eliminating any tip up when locking the fence in place. The plastic sight for the tape measure has a

small magnifying lens cast into it that made it difficult for me to read the tape.

The DeWalt fence utilizes a three-point clamping system at the front rail and a support rail at the back of the saw, which results in reliably parallel travel to the blade as the fence is moved. Setting the fence square to the table and parallel to the blade (and miter-gauge slots) requires loosening the same three screws, and it took several tries before I got it square and parallel; however, once set, the fence was stout and had no side deflection. The aluminum extrusion that makes up the face of the fence can be removed and switched to the opposite side of the main fence beam, much like the Delta Unifence. Overall, I liked the Unifence for its versatility and the General fence for its bricks-and-mortar simplicity.

Motors Rated 1½ hp to 2 hp Are Sufficient

I made test cuts with all of these saws using 3-ft. and 4-ft. lengths of 8/4 white oak and hard maple, and none of the saws disappointed me. Four of them—the Bridgewood, Delta, Jet JWTS-10JF, and Powermatic—are powered by 1½-hp motors and cut through the hardwood with relative ease. With each machine, however, the feed rate was fairly slow. The Jet SuperSaw and the DeWalt have 1¾-hp motors, and I could feel the difference in power when compared with the 1½-hp machines. I was able to use a slightly faster feed rate, and the motors didn't bog down quite as quickly under load. The General, Grizzly, and Woodtek saws have 2-hp motors, and the increased power was even more obvious.

Keeping a sawblade spinning at full speed is critical to the operation of most sawblades. As the blade slows due to lack of power or a feed rate that's too fast, the teeth do not cut as efficiently and excessive heat builds up at the rim of the blade. The heat causes the rim to expand slightly, forcing the blade to wobble, which can burn the wood and even damage the motor. Remedies for this problem are more horsepower, a blade with a thinner kerf, or simply raising the blade to increase the cutting angle.

Switches Should Be Easily Accessible

I used to have an older version of the Delta contractor's saw that had a toggle switch located low on the front of the saw—placed there to prevent the user from turning it on unintentionally—but it was difficult to turn

off the saw in a hurry. Manufacturers now make switches that are easy to use and logically placed—great not only for convenience but also for safety.

DeWalt's switch is large and well placed and can be shut down with your knee when both hands are needed elsewhere. The Jet SuperSaw has a push-button switch with an oversize off button and a location that makes it easy to use your knee to deactivate the saw. Delta's switch is well placed and can be pressed by hand or knee. The Jet JWTS-10JF, Powermatic, and General use identical push-button switches that are logically placed and easy to reach.

The Woodtek and Bridgewood use the same push-button switch as the Jet, Powermatic, General, and Grizzly, but it extends far enough out from the front rail that you can shut off the saw accidentally by leaning against the switch at the end of a rip cut.

Left-Tilting Trunnions Make Most Miter Rips Safer

Ripping miters on a tablesaw is the safest when performed with the sawblade tilted away from the fence. To make a miter rip-cut on right-tilting saws, such as the Delta, Grizzly, Jet JWTS-10JF, and Woodtek (which also offers a left-tilt version), the fence must be moved to the left of the sawblade, limiting the width of cut. A blade that tilts to the left eliminates this problem.

Stops for the tilt mechanism are adjustable on all of these saws. The stops positively locate 90° and 45° blade settings. Allen-head screws located in the tabletop make it easy to set the stops on the Delta and DeWalt. Delta locates the screws in the tabletop, while DeWalt locates them in the miter-gauge slots.

Dust Collection Is Limited

Containing the dust on any contractor-style saw is difficult because the back of the saw cabinet is open to allow the drive belt and the tilt mechanism to function.

JET JWTS-10JF

The Jet was a good-quality machine with a reliable fence. There was a lot of attention to detail, but the machine was more expensive than most of the other saws.

Street price	$899
Motor	1½ hp/18 amp at 120 V
Blade tilt	Right
Maximum rip capacity	30 in.
Runout at rim of 10-in. testing disc	0.002 in.
Blade alignment	0.004 in. out of parallel
Dust collection	Tray in base of saw cabinet with 4-in.-diameter outlet

POWERMATIC 64A

The blade was out of parallel with the miter slot, and the factory 45° tilt setting was off by several degrees. Both can be adjusted, but at $899 it's fair to expect everything to be set accurately at the factory.

Street price	$899
Motor	1½ hp/15 amp at 120 V
Blade tilt	Left
Maximum rip capacity	30⅜ in.
Runout at rim of 10-in. testing disc	0.003 in.
Blade alignment	0.004 in. out of parallel
Dust collection	Tray in base of saw cabinet with 4-in.-diameter outlet

The Delta has a metal pan—part of the base support—that angles down toward the back of the saw, directing most of the sawdust into a pile behind the stand. This design makes it easier to sweep up the saw-dust pile, but it does nothing to trap fine, airborne dust.

The Bridgewood, General, Grizzly, Jet JWTS-10JF, Powermatic, and Woodtek saws each has a plastic tray with a 4-in.-diameter outlet in the middle that covers the bottom of the saw cabinet. This system allows easy hookup to a dust-collection system, but because the back of the saw is still wide open, the dust collection is marginal.

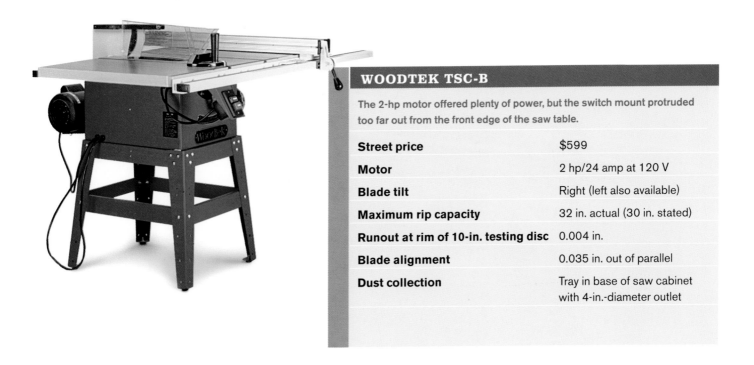

WOODTEK TSC-B

The 2-hp motor offered plenty of power, but the switch mount protruded too far out from the front edge of the saw table.

Street price	$599
Motor	2 hp/24 amp at 120 V
Blade tilt	Right (left also available)
Maximum rip capacity	32 in. actual (30 in. stated)
Runout at rim of 10-in. testing disc	0.004 in.
Blade alignment	0.035 in. out of parallel
Dust collection	Tray in base of saw cabinet with 4-in.-diameter outlet

Jet's SuperSaw has a steel tray in the bottom of the cabinet that is perforated to allow dust to be extracted from the cabinet through a 4-in.-diameter outlet. A plastic tray below the perforated tray acts as a catch-all and seals the system for dust extraction.

The blade shroud (below the table) on the DeWalt was effective at containing the dust around the blade, but the outlet has only a 2¼-in.-diameter opening and is immediately routed into a 90° elbow, which reduces the dust-collection efficiency. Also, the combination of a small outlet and a quick turn in the pipe can result in small offcuts plugging up the opening. The back and the bottom of the saw cabinet are open, so the blade shroud is responsible for all of the dust collection. The system probably would be more effective with a larger collection port.

Guards and Splitters Could Use Some Improvement

All of these saws come equipped with a splitter with anti-kickback pawls combined with a blade guard. These devices are mounted in one of two locations: on a

bar off the back of the saw or onto a fitting right behind the blade, under the table insert. With most of these assemblies, you can fold the guard out of the way when you need to change the blade. The design of the Delta guard is slightly different. It has a notched section on the back of the clear plastic guard that is supposed to hook onto the metal splitter, but I couldn't get it to stay upright (useful if you wish to measure the blade height) without removing the table insert. The Powermatic has a design in which there are two independently pivoting guards on both sides of the blade. Those guards are held by a frame that sits above the splitter, and that frame is riveted to the splitter, so you cannot move the guards out of the way without removing the entire splitter assembly. The DeWalt has the most workable design of them all—a smaller assembly that mounts only to one location, into the trunnion right behind the saw-blade. In the case of the DeWalt, smaller and simpler made it better.

Features to Consider

SWITCHES

THIS BIG SWITCH IS EASY TO FIND. The DeWalt switch is conveniently located and easy to turn off with your knee if your hands are busy elsewhere.

DUST COLLECTION

A CHUTE FOR DIRECTING SAWDUST. The Delta saw has an angled pan that sends sawdust out the back of the machine, which, unfortunately, allows fine dust to escape and become airborne.

AN ACCESS DOOR AND A PERFORATED TRAY. The Jet SuperSaw has a fairly airtight base, accessed through a hinged door. Johnson thinks the tray with holes in it on the Jet SuperSaw will work well with fine sawdust, but he found that some dadoing and ripping operations will cause it to clog up.

All of the Saws Performed Acceptably

Any one of these saws would be welcome in my shop. But if I had to choose just one from this batch, it would be the General for a variety of reasons. It has plenty of power (with that 2-hp motor), a simple and reliable fence, and little things (such as the mounted hangers for the rip and crosscut fences) that suggest an attention to detail. And though it's not the least expensive, the price is well below that of many of the other machines.

As a second choice, I would pick the DeWalt because I really liked its heavier trunnions and arbor casting. If the dust collection were modified a bit, I could easily find a spot in my shop for that big yellow saw.

*Please note price estimates are from 2004.

ROLAND JOHNSON builds custom cabinetry and architectural millwork in a shop near St. Cloud, Minn.

Hybrid Saws

Hybrid saws are a cross between the older style contractor's saws and the heavier-duty standard cabinet saws. Design features on these two saws vary somewhat (see details below). For both the DeWalt and the Jet hybrid saws, you also can purchase sliding-table assemblies as optional accessories. Hybrids may represent the future direction of contractor-style saws.

DEWALT DW746

The trunnions and arbor on this saw were heavier than those on the other saws. Its compact footprint would be nice for the small shop. Dust collection would be more effective with a larger outlet.

Street price	$849
Motor	1¾ hp/15 amp at 120 V
Blade tilt	Left
Maximum rip capacity	30⅝ in.
Runout at rim of 10-in. testing disc	0.003 in.
Blade alignment	0.000 in. out of parallel
Dust collection	Blade shroud in base of saw cabinet with attachment for 2¼-in.-diameter vacuum hose

JET JWSS-10LFR

The saw was equipped with the same arbor and trunnions as the Jet contractor-style saw but with a new motor location and a great drive-belt system. The fence had a sight glass that was hard to read from some angles and a rubber thumbwheel for fine-tuning the fence setting.

Street price	$849
Motor	1¾ hp/12 amp at 120 V
Blade tilt	Left
Maximum rip capacity	33 in.
Runout at rim of 10-in. testing disc	0.003 in.
Blade alignment	0.035 in. out of parallel
Dust collection	Collection tray in cabinet base with 4-in.-diameter outlet

Ten-Inch Combination Tablesaw Blades

BY TOM BEGNAL

OUR HIGH-TECH TEST of 14 new blades revealed the smoothest cutters

A combination blade for the tablesaw makes good sense for many woodworkers. Although a combination blade, also called a general-purpose blade, might not rip as well as a rip blade or crosscut as well as a crosscut blade, it can come pretty close. And using one means you won't have to switch back and forth from rip to crosscut blade. That makes life a lot easier in the shop.

As anyone in the market for a combination blade soon discovers, there's no shortage of choices. That's true even in the top-of-the-line category I wanted to look at. Indeed, 14 of these blades are commonly available.

Curious to learn whether any of these blue bloods stood out from one another, I decided to test all 14 in the *Fine Woodworking* shop (for a complete list of the blades, see the chart on p. 21). But before doing that, I had to consider what exactly I was testing. After all, a combination blade has to do just two things well: make smooth cuts and go a reasonable length of time between sharpenings. So first I needed to figure out whether I wanted to focus on smoothness of cut, on wear, or on both.

My ultimate choice was based on a couple of factors. In a preliminary test,

Why Tablesaw Blades Get Dull

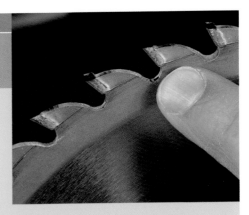

PITCH IS A PROBLEM. A heavy buildup of pitch on sawblade teeth can lead to poor cutting and shorter blade life.

Like any cutting tool, a tablesaw blade gets dull as it is used. And it can become dull for any of several reasons or some combination of them all.

Wear is certainly one reason why a blade gets dull. As each tooth slices through wood, the cutting edge slowly abrades until it no longer cuts as cleanly or easily as it once did.

That's why blades with carbide-tipped teeth are usually favored over high-speed steel (HSS) teeth. Carbide teeth are harder, so they don't wear as easily as blades with HSS teeth. Indeed, some manufacturers claim that teeth made from carbide can last 15 times longer than those made from HSS.

PITCH BUILDUP

Another culprit is pitch buildup. As a blade cuts through wood, some of the resins in the wood stick to the teeth. Those resins can build up to a point that the blade can't cut as smoothly.

Resin buildup also causes the cutting edge of each tooth to run hotter than normal. This is a particular concern for carbide-tipped blades, because each tooth is actually just a bunch of tiny grains of carbide held together by a material, called a binder, that acts like glue. When a blade runs hot, the binder begins to weaken, allowing some of the grains to break away.

Resins can cause problems in still another way. Chemicals in some resins can react with the binder and break it down, again causing grains of carbide to disappear.

NAILS AND OTHER METAL IN WOOD

Because of its hardness, carbide is a great material for tablesaw-blade teeth. But that hardness comes at the cost of brittleness. Granted, brittleness isn't usually a problem when cutting wood. But when carbide teeth have unintentional run-ins with steel, the teeth come away either cracked or chipped. So be sure to remove any nails or screws from a board before cutting.

A tablesaw blade doesn't have to be spinning to encounter a problem.

Once, while changing a blade, I chipped a carbide tooth by accidentally hitting it with the arbor-nut wrench.

WHAT TO DO

Because pitch buildup has the potential to be a three-way problem, it makes good sense to regularly clean off any pitch that shows up on your sawblade.

Beyond that, it's mostly a matter of keeping the teeth away from nails, screws and free-swinging wrenches. In the end, your blade is going to enjoy a long time between visits to the resharpening shop.

---

using a tablesaw with a 10-in. carbide-tipped combination blade, I was able to cut 2,000 linear ft. of ⅜-in.-thick Baltic birch plywood before the blade began to show even the slightest sign of wear. Then too, in my research on blades, I came across a test done several years ago at Pittsburg State University in Pittsburg, Kansas, where four carbide-tipped tablesaw blades each cut between 4,000 linear ft. and 6,000 linear ft. of ¾-in.-thick plywood. For most home shops, those kinds of numbers represent years of wear. So as a practical matter, it made sense simply to test for smoothness of cut.

Preparing the Sample Blocks

TABLESAW SETUP

Sample blocks (below) had to be cut before any test for smoothness could be done. To create them, each blade cut a 2-in. square block from ¾-in.-thick straight-grained soft maple.

To ensure consistent tablesaw cuts, a dial indicator helped align the blade and rip fence with the miter-gauge slot (right). A power feeder (below right) maintained the same feed rate during rip cuts.

Blade #4
Cross cut ^
Rip ∨

CUTTING THE BLOCKS

Positioning the power feeder behind the tablesaw insert (right) allowed Begnal to change blades without having to reposition the feeder each time. Once ripped, it took just a couple of crosscuts (below), sans power feeder, to produce each sample block. Handplaning the edge opposite the sawn edge (below right) allowed Begnal to measure and compare the relative smoothness of both edges.

HANDPLANING. The edge opposite the sawn edge of each block was handplaned flat. Both surfaces were measured to help account for any differences in the grain of each sample block.

Measuring the Results

HOW THE MACHINE SCORED THE CUTS

To measure deviations in the cut surfaces of the sample blocks, the team used a surface roughness and profiling system. The machine can measure remarkably small surface deviations. As the stylus slid along the surface of a sample block, a digital readout of the ups and downs appeared on a computer screen. The readouts below represent the average of at least three passes by the stylus. Each horizontal line on each readout represents just over 0.0004 in.

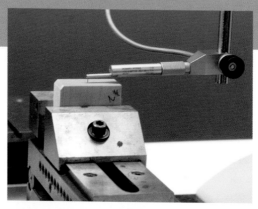

MACHINE AND WOOD MEET AT THE STYLUS. The machine slowly dragged a stylus across the cut edge, measuring smoothness as it went along.

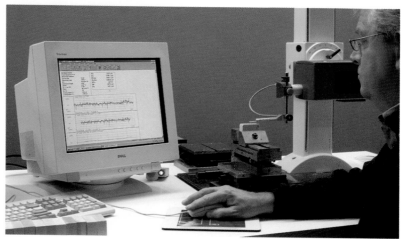

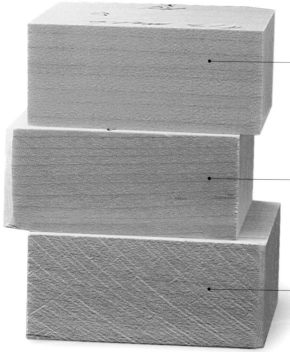

A RIP-CUT SURFACE AFTER HANDPLANING

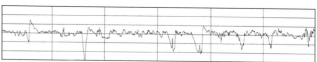

A RIP CUT RATED EXCELLENT

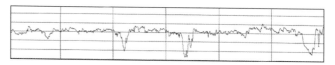

A RIP CUT RATED FAIR

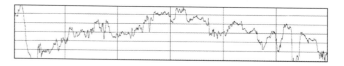

To test each new blade, I first ripped and crosscut a ¾-in.-thick maple board to produce a 2-in.-square sample. After that, the ripped and crosscut edges on each sample were checked for smoothness on a high-tech machine. Then the general quality of each cut was categorized. To keep the test as controlled as possible, I didn't include thin-kerfed blades. Also, no stiffening collars were used. One other point: Blades sometimes dull faster than they ought to. Chances are, factors other than pure tooth-to-wood wear are responsible. For more about premature wear, plus some tips on keeping blades sharper longer, see "Why Tablesaw Blades Get Dull" on p. 15.

Cutting the Sample Pieces

For consistency and accuracy, the tablesaw setup was critical (see the photos on p. 16). The blade and the rip fence had to be perfectly parallel to the miter-gauge slot. That meant doing some measuring with a dial indicator, with the final check made as the rip fence was positioned for the required 2-in. rip cut.

Also, I added a power feeder to the tablesaw to ensure that all of the test rip cuts were made at the same speed. The power feeder was positioned behind the tablesaw insert so that the blades could be changed and the crosscuts made without having to reposition the feeder. That proved helpful, because it's difficult to reset a power feeder without affecting the cut to some degree.

Because there was no practical way to crosscut the samples using the power feeder, those cuts were made using hand power and a miter gauge (see the top right photo on p. 16). And although it's pretty much impossible to cut by hand and get the same feed rate every single time, I made a conscious effort to keep them as close as possible.

I used soft maple for the test samples, and it took some serious searching through several stacks of lumber to find a few boards with grain that was reasonably straight. But it was worth the effort, because using straight-grained wood for all of the cuts helped add consistency to the test.

Next, to prepare the samples for the test, I planed each one to the same ¾-in. thickness. Then I jointed the long edges before cutting the samples to 4-ft. lengths.

At this point, a new combination blade was installed in the tablesaw, with the height of the blade set so the gullet cleared the top face of the board by ¼ in. To avoid confusing the test edge with the edge placed against the rip fence, I ran a marker down the entire length of the edge that registered against the fence. Then, with the power feeder adjusted for a cutting rate of 15 ft. per minute, the board was ripped to a 2-in. width.

Next, at a point 1 ft. from the back end (the end that last went through the power feeder), the ripped piece was crosscut twice. The first cut was a trimming cut; the second one created the 2-in. test square. On the top of the sample I marked both the rip and crosscut edges to be analyzed.

After crosscutting the sample, I used a sharp handplane to smooth the opposite edges of each sample (see the bottom right photo on p. 17). I'll explain why a bit later.

To complete the preparation, the sample was placed in a resealable plastic bag. The bag added some abrasion protection, but more important, it kept ambient moisture away from the wood. Any drying or dampening of the wood could have affected the surface quality before the tests were complete. This entire procedure was repeated for each of the 14 blades.

Measuring the Surface Smoothness

To get an objective measure of how smooth a cut each blade made, I enlisted the help of Hommel America, a company in New Britain, Connecticut, specializing in sophisticated equipment for checking smoothness. The machine used, called a surface roughness and profiling system, can measure remarkably small surface deviations (see the photos on p. 18). For example, on a highly polished surface, such as an automotive crankshaft journal, the machine can measure deviations as tiny as plus or minus one-hundredth of a micro-inch. (A micro-inch, by the way, is one millionth of an inch.) But for a relatively rough material, like the wood samples, the machine was scaled back to measure ± 1,250 micro-in., or 0.00125 in.

To do the test, each wood sample was clamped to a special fixture on the machine, then a delicate measuring device called a stylus was pulled across the surface. And, as the cone-shaped, diamond-tipped stylus moved, it followed every little hill and valley on the surface. It also generated on a computer screen a digital readout that showed the up-and-down travel of the stylus. At the same time, it computed a number that represents the average roughness of the surface. The lower the number, the smoother the surface.

At that point, it might have been tempting just to measure each sawn edge and compare the results. But the test needed to go one step further, because wood is a natural material, which means no two pieces are exactly alike. Concerned that this could skew the results, we measured each sawn surface against the surface on the opposite edge that was handplaned earlier.

Effectively, then, for each sample, we measured the smoothest possible surface for a particular sample (the handplaned edge) against the actual sawn cut. Therefore, as much as possible, this approach eliminated the natural differences in the various samples of wood. And as a result, I had a much fairer set of numbers to use when making an evaluation.

One more point. When crosscutting, it's not unusual to get some splintering on the edges of the wood. It's called tearout, and good tablesaw blades keep it to a minimum. Although the tests didn't directly measure tearout, we found that sawblades that made smoother crosscuts tended to produce less tearout.

The Smoothest Performers

After looking at the test results, it was clear that some blades were smoother cutters than others (see the chart on the facing page). Of the 14 blades, the Forrest proved to be the smoothest of the bunch. It was the only one to earn an excellent rating in both the rip and crosscut categories. At $119, it's one of the pricier models, but the test suggests that it's money well spent.

The sawblades from Everlast, Jesada, and U.S. Saw (the newest blade from Oldham®) cut almost as well as the Forrest, getting ratings of very good and excellent. When price is factored in, Everlast enjoys some added appeal in that it sells for about 40 percent less than the Forrest blade.

Vermont American's® blade also received honor marks, scoring a very good rating in both categories. It's about the same price as the Everlast blade.

★Please note price estimates are from 2004.

TOM BEGNAL is an associate editor of *Fine Woodworking*.

Rating the Blades

Based on the machine measurements, the smoothness of each rip and crosscut was rated as excellent, very good, good, or fair. Forrest graduated magna cum laude here, capturing an excellent score for both ripping and crosscutting. Everlast, Jesada and U.S Saw also garnered high honors.

RATING THE BLADES

Blade	Price	Rip Cut	Crosscut
Amana PR1040 (800) 445-0077	$85	Very good	Good
CMT® 213.040.10 (888) 268-2487	$55	Good	Good
Craftsman® 26789 (800) 697-3277	$35	Fair	Very good
DeWalt DW7615 (800) 433-9258	$69	Good	Very good
DML 74010 (800) 242-7003	$66	Good	Very good
Everlast AGP1040 (800) 387-5278	$70	Excellent	Very good
Forrest Woodworker II WW10407125 (800) 733-7111	$119	Excellent	Excellent
Freud® F410 (800) 334-4107	$95	Good	Very Good
Jesada 110-440 (800) 531-5559	$90	Excellent	Very good
Ridge TS2000 (800) 443-0992	$119	Good	Very good
Systimatic 1030 (800) 426-0035	$50	Fair	Good
Tenryu® GM-25540 (800) 951-7297	$95	Very good	Good
U.S. Saw (Oldham) 100W40 (800) 828-9000	$60	Excellent	Very good
Vermont American 27656 (800) 742-3869	$75	Very good	Very good

A Tablesaw Primer: Ripping and Crosscutting

BY KELLY MEHLER

With its flat, circular spinning blade doing the hard work, the tablesaw can make all sorts of cuts, among them grooves, dadoes, rabbets, and a variety of other woodworking joints. However, the tablesaw most commonly is called on to do just two basic tasks: make wide boards narrower, a process called ripping, and make long boards shorter, a process called crosscutting. When ripping, the rip fence is used to guide the stock. Crosscutting is done with the aid of the miter gauge.

Because so much tablesaw run time is spent ripping and crosscutting, it's especially important to have good work habits while making these two fundamental cuts. After all, when used properly, a good tablesaw can produce remarkably smooth and accurate cuts safely and with little effort.

The Saw Must Be Set up Properly for Best Results

A tablesaw won't cut easily, accurately, or safely if it's improperly set up. So before making any rip cut or crosscut, make sure the saw is in good working order and properly adjusted. Also, the table of the saw should be flat, with any deviation limited to no more than 0.010 in. The same goes for any extension tables. And when assembled, those tables all should be flush.

Then, too, the sawblade should be sharp. A sharp combination blade can produce good cuts when ripping and crosscutting.

Use the blade cover, splitter, and pawls

The saw must have a blade guard that includes a cover, splitter, and pawls. Granted, such a guard system isn't a foolproof device, but it does improve safety. The cover itself acts as a barrier, helping block any misdirected hand or finger from contacting the spinning blade. That's a big plus. Also, the splitter and pawls minimize the chance of kickback or ejection.

Kickback occurs most often during a rip cut, usually when the workpiece twists away from the rip fence just enough to contact the teeth on the back portion of the blade; those are the teeth just coming up through the insert after traveling under the saw. When that happens, those back teeth can grab the workpiece, lifting it and instantly launching it, usually right back at the operator. But a splitter behind the blade helps prevent the workpiece from contacting the back teeth, so kickback is less likely to happen.

Ejection occurs most often when ripping a relatively narrow piece, just after the sawblade cuts the piece free. At that point,

The Parts of the Tablesaw

Most tablesaws have similar types of controls and accessories, no matter if they are small benchtop units, contractor's saws (shown), or heavy-duty, floor-standing cabinet machines.

Tablesaw Setup

Before making a cut, make sure the machine is properly set up. The rip fence, the tablesaw blade, and the miter-gauge slots must be parallel to one other.

Blade

Rip fence

Miter-gauge slot

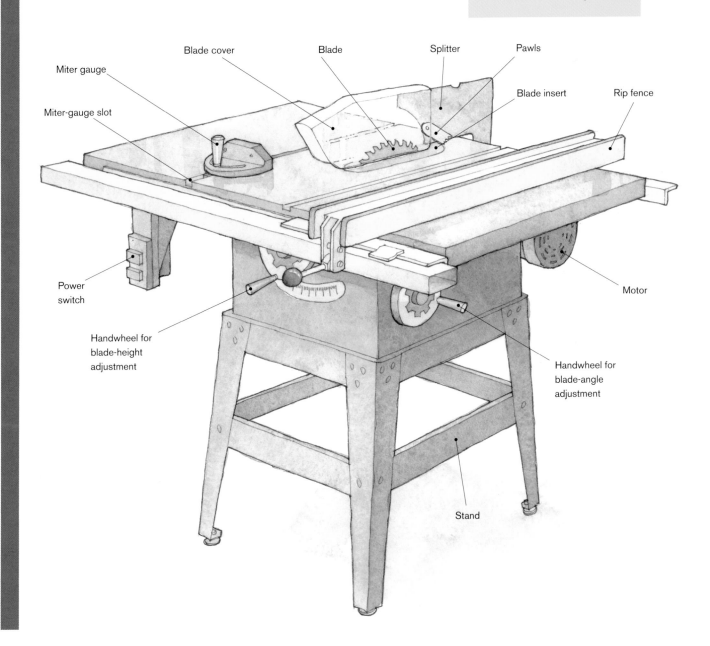

Miter gauge

Blade cover

Blade

Splitter

Pawls

Miter-gauge slot

Blade insert

Rip fence

Power switch

Handwheel for blade-height adjustment

Motor

Handwheel for blade-angle adjustment

Stand

Essential Accessories

Tablesaws come from the factory with everything needed to start making rip cuts and crosscuts. But a few important accessories improve both the safety and accuracy of the saw.

Outfeed support table

Push Blocks

When making a rip cut 8 in. wide or less, a push block or push stick is a must. It's an extension of your hand, so your fingers stay a reasonably safe distance from the blade. A push stick is effective for pushing a board, but it holds down little more than the trailing end. I prefer a push block (above) because it provides downward pressure along more than just the end. That way, the board is less likely to flutter and, more important, is less susceptible to kickback. It takes just a few minutes to make a push block. Use any ¾-in.- or 1-in.-thick stock and cut it to shape with a bandsaw or sabersaw.

Push Block

Outfeed Support

There's not much distance between the back of the blade and the back of the saw table. As a result, boards can end up falling off the back of the saw at the end of a cut. Also, when ripping a long board, you must bear down hard to prevent it from tipping off the back at the end of the cut. That's not something you want to do with your hand passing near the blade. So it's important to have some sort of auxiliary support at the back of the saw. A sturdy table is best, but even a support stand will help.

Zero-Clearance Insert

When a tablesaw comes from the factory, the blade insert typically has a wide opening. That's fine for bevel cuts or wide rip cuts. But for a narrow rip cut, the trailing end of the piece can drop down through the opening in the insert. As the piece tips, your pushing hand follows it. And you don't want your hand to drop toward a spinning sawblade. If that's not scary enough, you run the risk of kickback, too. To avoid those problems, I use a zero-clearance insert for almost all of my cuts. Most woodworking mail-order catalogs sell inserts made from phenolic plastic and precut to fit most any make and model of saw. Or you can cut your own from plywood.

The wide slot of a factory insert can trap thin stock.

The narrow slot of a zero-clearance insert is created by raising the blade through the insert.

if the piece tips, twists, or bends, it can become pinched between the blade and the rip fence. And if the piece is not supported by a push block or pawls, the force of the spinning blade can send the piece straight back at warp speed. Indeed, I've seen photos of a ¾-in.-sq. by 4-ft.-long piece that shot back 6 ft. and fully penetrated a sheet of ¾-in.-thick plywood.

Flat, Square Stock Is a Must

A warped board or a board with uneven edges can be difficult to control when ripping or crosscutting. Such boards are likely to rock during a cut. When that happens, the wood binds against the side of the blade. At best, you end up with a rough edge that isn't square. At worst, you get kickback or ejection (see the drawings on p. 26).

Before you make any tablesaw cuts, check that the face surfaces of the board are flat. Also, any edge that will meet the rip fence or the miter gauge must be straight. If the flat surface or straight edge is missing, the stock needs to be hand-planed or jointed.

How to Avoid Kickback or Ejection while Ripping

Smooth rip cuts can become routine if you follow a few basic cutting techniques. Not only will you get smooth rip cuts but you'll also be able to get them with a better degree of safety. That's important, especially when you consider that most tablesaw accidents occur during rip cuts. A safety point: Don't rip a board that is wider than it is long. With the shortest edge of the board bearing against the rip fence, the

board easily can twist away from the fence and into the side of the blade, an invitation to kickback.

When you're faced with making a narrow rip cut, typically one that's between 1¼ in. wide and 3 in. wide, the blade cover usually ends up interfering with your right hand as you use the push block to feed the board through the blade. To avoid that problem, use a tall push block, which puts your hand well above the cover as the stock is pushed along.

For the narrowest rip cuts, between ⅛ in. wide and 1¼ in. wide, use a notched sled when the stock is less than about 24 in. long (see the drawing on p. 27). A handle on top helps you push the sled while making sure the edge of the sled stays against the rip fence. To set the width of the cut, simply measure the distance from the sled's inside edge to the sawblade's inside edge. For longer parts that require a narrow rip cut, clamp a short auxiliary fence to the rip fence. The short fence allows the stock to slide under the blade cover. However, when the front of the push block reaches the cover, you'll have to stop pushing and go to the back of the saw. The pawls will keep the stock in place. Once at the back, you can complete the final few inches of the cut by pulling the narrow piece through the blade.

Use a Firm Grip while Crosscutting

The most common crosscut is made with the miter gauge set at 90° to the miter-gauge slot, resulting in a square cut. However, consistently smooth, square crosscuts don't happen automatically. You need to follow a few basic procedures.

When making rip cuts, stand to the left of the blade with your left hip against the front rail.

Keep the push block close at hand.

Feed the stock with your right hand, keeping your right arm in line with the board.

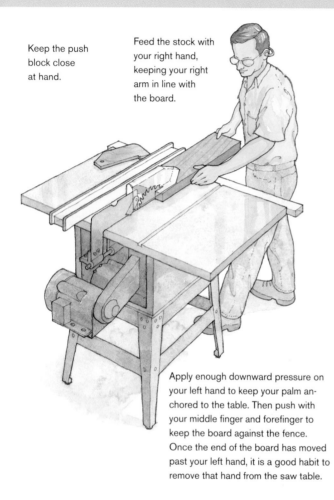

Apply enough downward pressure on your left hand to keep your palm anchored to the table. Then push with your middle finger and forefinger to keep the board against the fence. Once the end of the board has moved past your left hand, it is a good habit to remove that hand from the saw table.

Avoiding Ejection and Kickback

Ejection occurs when a cutoff piece gets pinched between the blade and the rip fence. If the piece is not supported by a push block or pawls, it can shoot straight back. Kickback occurs when a workpiece twists into the upward-spinning blade teeth. The teeth can launch the piece at your nose in an instant.

Stand clear of the ejection zone—the area between the fence and blade.

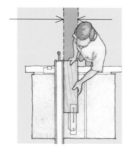

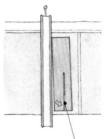

With a splitter behind the blade, kickback is less likely to occur because the workpiece can't easily contact the back teeth of the blade.

A SIMPLE RIP CUT

Most tablesaw accidents occur during ripping. By following a few basic techniques, not only will you get good-quality cuts but you'll also get them with a better degree of safety.

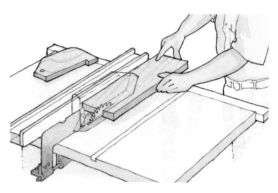

1 Place the front end of the board on the saw. Then, with the edge of the board against the rip fence, feed the board into the blade at a steady rate. If the motor slows down, slow the feed rate.

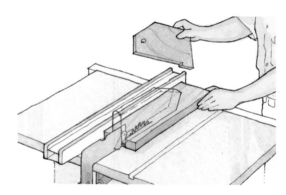

2 Once the trailing end of the board reaches the front of the table, use the push block to feed the board.

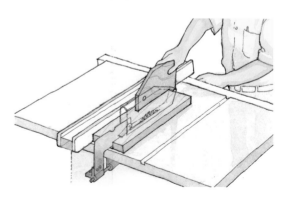

3 Continue pushing the trailing end of the board with the push block until the board is an inch or two past the sawblade.

RIPPING NARROW BOARDS

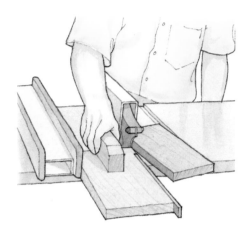

When ripping parts less than about 1¼ in. wide, use a notched sled, guided by the rip fence, to push the stock through the blade. A handle makes for easier pushing.

A shopmade L-shaped fence mounted to the rip fence creates extra space between the blade cover and the rip fence, making it easier to feed the stock, especially when a tall push block is used.

RIPPING LARGE PANELS

Full-size (4-ft. by 8-ft.) sheets of plywood and other sheet goods are heavy and awkward to handle, which make them a chore to cut. But with a little forethought and practice, the procedure can be reasonably straightforward.

1 Place the leading edge of the sheet on the front of the saw with the back end resting on the floor.

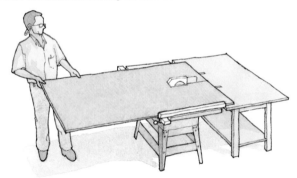

2 Stand at the left corner of the sheet with your body more alongside the left edge than the end. From that position it's easier to hold the edge of the sheet against the rip fence. When making the cut, both arms should be comfortably outstretched with your left arm along the left edge and your right arm on the end.

3 As you feed the sheet and begin to approach the front of the saw, shift your body more to the front of the sheet. Once at the front of the table, assume your normal starting stance to complete the cut. Have a helper support the end of the sheet.

Crosscutting

The starting position for a square crosscut is about the same as the one used for ripping. Stand in front of the miter gauge with your left hip against the front rail.

Hold the board against the miter-gauge fence with your left hand. For safety, keep fingers at least 6 in. from the blade cover.

Use your right hand to push the gauge toward the back of the saw.

The miter gauge works just as well in either of the two miter slots. But because most people are right-handed, the majority of tablesaw users push the miter gauge with their right hand, so the gauge has to go into the left slot.

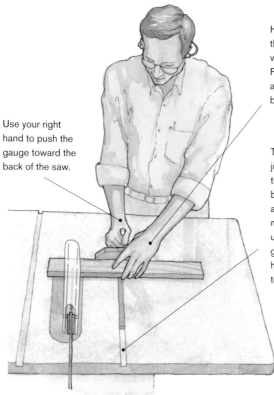

Use An Auxiliary Fence to Crosscut Long Boards

A typical miter-gauge fence is relatively short, so it doesn't offer a lot of support to long boards. An easy solution is to screw a long auxiliary wood fence to the miter-gauge fence. You can make the wood fence to any length, but just be sure it's flat and straight.

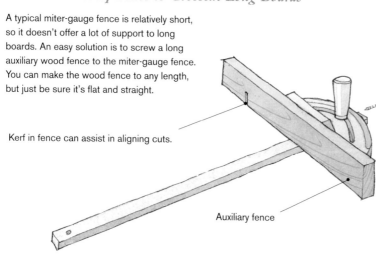

Kerf in fence can assist in aligning cuts.

Auxiliary fence

A SIMPLE CROSSCUT

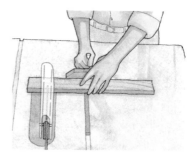

1 Keep the board away from the blade (an inch or two) before starting the saw. Push the miter gauge with your right hand, feeding the board at a steady speed. Stop pushing after the cut but continue to hold the board against the fence.

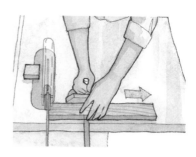

2 To avoid having the spinning blade touch the cut edge of the board when the miter gauge is pulled back to the starting position, possibly causing a little extra splintering, it's best to shift the board away from the blade slightly.

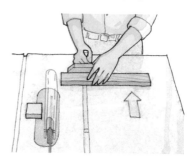

3 While holding the board against the fence, pull both the board and the gauge back to the starting position. Then shut off the saw.

REPEAT CUTS FOR LONG PARTS

When you're cutting several boards to the same length, a stop block clamped to the auxiliary miter-gauge fence will ensure uniformity. First, cut one end square on each piece. After that, clamp the stop block to the fence, making sure the distance from the block to the blade matches the length you want. Then, one piece at a time, butt the square end of the board against the block and make the cut.

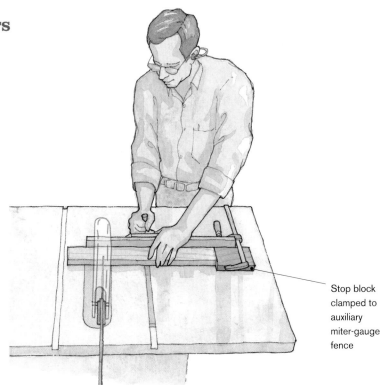

Stop block clamped to auxiliary miter-gauge fence

REPEAT CUTS FOR SHORT PARTS

To save time, clamp a stop block to the rip fence when you need to cut several short pieces of wood to the same length. Position the fence so that the distance from the block to the blade equals the needed length measurement. To avoid binding the cutoff piece between the blade and the stop block, which could cause kickback, the block must be far enough in front of the blade so that the board isn't touching the block during the cut.

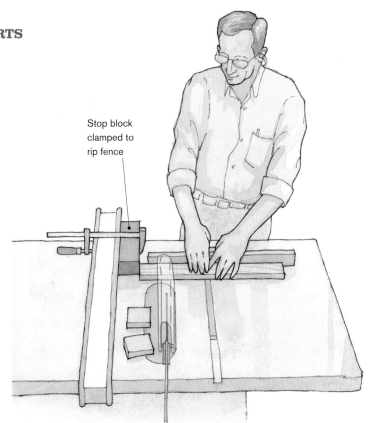

Stop block clamped to rip fence

Position the board on the miter gauge

Place the board on the saw table. Use your left hand to hold the board against the miter-gauge fence and slide the gauge forward with your right hand until the leading edge of the board almost touches the blade. At this point, use one or two hands as needed to align the sawblade with the cut line on the board.

Push the board through the blade When everything is aligned, use your left hand to hold the board firmly against the miter-gauge fence until the cut is completed. The holding force you apply should be straight back, and your fingers should be at least 6 in. from the blade cover. Slide the board an inch or two away from the blade before starting the saw. Use your right hand to push the gauge toward the back of the saw, and feed the board at a steady speed. Stop pushing once the cut is finished, but continue to hold the board firmly against the miter-gauge fence.

Pull back the board Once the board has been cut, continue to hold the board firmly against the fence, and pull both the board and the gauge back to the starting position. Once back to the starting point, you can relax your hold on the board and shut off the saw.

Oftentimes, as the board and miter gauge are pulled back, the spinning blade will slightly touch the cut edge of the board and cause a little extra splintering. To avoid the problem—and if the board is small and light enough—I'll use my left hand to shift the board ⅛ in. to ¼ in. away from the blade before pulling it back. Bigger and heavier boards, however, won't move as easily. So if I'm cutting a big board while in splinter-phobic mode, I simply shut off the saw before removing the board and pulling back the gauge.

Add a stop block to the rip fence when cutting several short pieces to the same length It's not uncommon to need several short pieces of wood, each one the same length. When that's the case, I clamp a stop block to the rip fence. Then the fence is positioned so that the distance from the block to the blade equals the length measurement I need. To avoid kickback, the block must be far enough from the blade so that the board isn't touching the block when it starts being cut by the blade.

Add a stop block to the auxiliary miter-gauge fence when cutting longer boards to the same length Make sure the distance from the block to the blade matches the length you want. First, though, using only the auxiliary fence, cut one end of each board square. Then butt the square end of each board against the block and cut one piece at a time.

Another versatile jig that gets a lot of use in my shop is the crosscut sled. The sled makes crosscutting even more accurate and safe.

Once you've mastered the basic techniques of ripping and crosscutting, you'll be ready to tackle the other various tasks suitable for the tablesaw, such as cutting miters, tenons, and tapers.

KELLY MEHLER is the author of *The Table Saw Book* (The Taunton Press, Inc., 2003). He lives in Berea, Ky.

Joint-Quality Edges Cut on a Tablesaw

When I tell my students that a lot of professional woodworkers use a tablesaw to get glue-ready edges, I sometimes hear gasps of disbelief. Most woodworkers think the tablesaw cuts crude, uneven edges, which must be cleaned up on a jointer. The assumption is that the smoother surface a jointer gives is better for glue, but this isn't always true. Glue must penetrate below the surface of the wood to do its job, so it needs open pores to seep in and grab hold. Jointer knives can compress the wood as they cut, glazing the surface and preventing maximum glue penetration—especially if the knives are dull or if the board is run over the jointer too slowly. However, running an edge over a jointer too fast cuts a pronounced wave pattern. If severe enough, only the tips will touch when two boards are put together, creating a wider glue line than is desirable.

The right technique on a tablesaw creates a straight, square and slightly abraded surface, which is ideal for glue joints. And a properly sawn edge, if it's to be left exposed, needs only light sanding to be finished. The trick is mostly in the way in which you feed the board through the cut. It has to move through the blade at a

A CLEAN JOINT LINE FRESH FROM THE TABLESAW. Sawn edges without further preparation can make perfectly good glue joints.

BY LON SCHLEINING

31

constant speed without wavering. All you need is a tablesaw with a powerful motor (3 hp or more), a good-quality triple-chip blade and an outfeed table. The rewards are great—less milling time for stronger glue joints and finished edges.

Two-Step at the Tablesaw

To cut a clean edge on a tablesaw, you'll need to rethink how you move the board over the saw, as well as how you move. The commonly accepted technique of standing next to the saw and feeding boards hand over hand ensures an uneven edge and, frankly, is a dangerous habit. There is a total reliance on friction between the hands and the top face of the board to feed it forward, hold it down on the table, and press it against the rip fence. The body is out of balance, and the hands (especially the left) move very close to the blade. One slip and the unthinkable might happen.

The following technique is a lot safer, but somewhat more complicated. It's very much like a bowling step. You need to coordinate your feet, hands and body into one fluid movement to ensure that the board goes over the saw steadily. I'll walk you through the technique, presuming that you have one edge of the board straight already. As you might have guessed, I straighten the first edge on the tablesaw instead of the jointer (see "Getting the First Edge Straight on a Tablesaw" on p. 36), but use whatever method suits you.

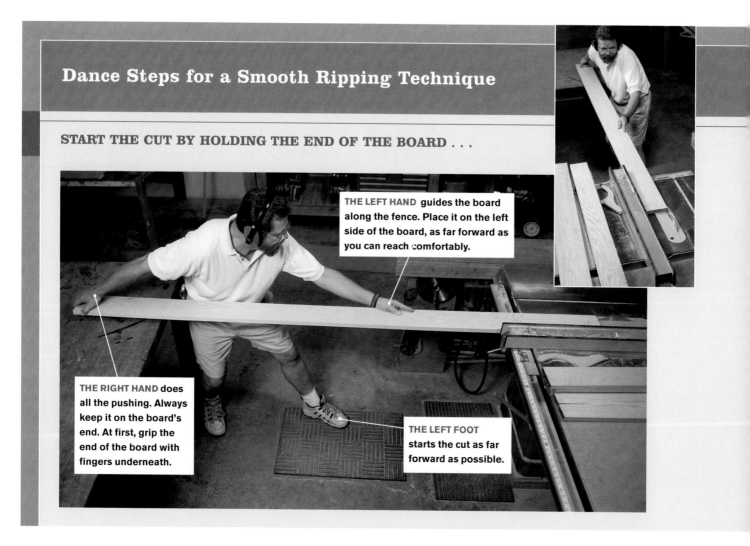

Dance Steps for a Smooth Ripping Technique

START THE CUT BY HOLDING THE END OF THE BOARD . . .

THE LEFT HAND guides the board along the fence. Place it on the left side of the board, as far forward as you can reach comfortably.

THE RIGHT HAND does all the pushing. Always keep it on the board's end. At first, grip the end of the board with fingers underneath.

THE LEFT FOOT starts the cut as far forward as possible.

The main focus of the technique is to keep the board moving safely and at a constant speed during the cut. This requires that you start and end the cut with your right hand pushing from the end of the board. Guide the board with your left hand, placing it as far forward on the board as you can comfortably.

Depending on how long the board is, you may need to start the cut standing a certain distance back from the saw and take a step or two toward the saw during the cut. This is when keeping the cut steady becomes more difficult, though by no means impossible. The key is to start with your left foot as far ahead of you as possible so that you need only take one smooth step with your right foot to reach the saw and finish the cut (the photos on pp. 34 and 35 show how to complete this movement).

A Triple-Chip Blade on a Powerful Saw

The right blade with this job, as for many things in life, is a compromise. In my experience, combination teeth can't remove material rapidly and produce a smooth edge. But pure rip grinds are often a bit too aggressive to cut cleanly. They remove material much faster than a combination grind but leave an edge that is too rough for gluing. Triple-chip grinds are less aggressive but remove material rapidly enough to provide the cleanest overall rip cut. However, beware of cheap triple-chip

LEAN INTO THE CUT, SHIFTING YOUR WEIGHT FORWARD . . .

THE LEFT HAND stops at the table edge, holds the board down and pushes it against the rip fence. Use the heel to help keep your balance.

THE LEFT FOOT starts to support most of the body's weight.

blades: I've found a range of quality among them that substantially affects performance.

Tablesaw setup is just as important as blade choice. The blade must run parallel to the fence. If it doesn't, you'll get a condition known as heel and toe, which can produce deep swirl cuts down the edge of the board. For ripping long boards, the hands of a well-intentioned helper are no substitute for a solid outfeed table. The smallest amount of lateral wandering from the line of cut will give you a less than perfect edge.

There is also no substitute for power to get the best edges. It's possible to do it with less than 3 hp, but lower horsepower machines have smaller sweet spots—the range of feed rates that a motor can handle without burning the edge or bogging down. The technique isn't impossible on a contractor's saw with a 1½-hp motor (I used one for years), but it's a lot harder.

If you push a board through any saw too fast, the motor will bog down and the blade will wobble, producing an uneven cut. But if you slow down too much, accumulated friction will burn the board. Both problems will leave you with a flawed edge. Higher horsepower motors can handle a wider range of feed rates—between burning at slow feed rates and bogging down at high feed rates. This makes it much easier to get a clean edge because you're not walking a tightrope between too slow and too fast.

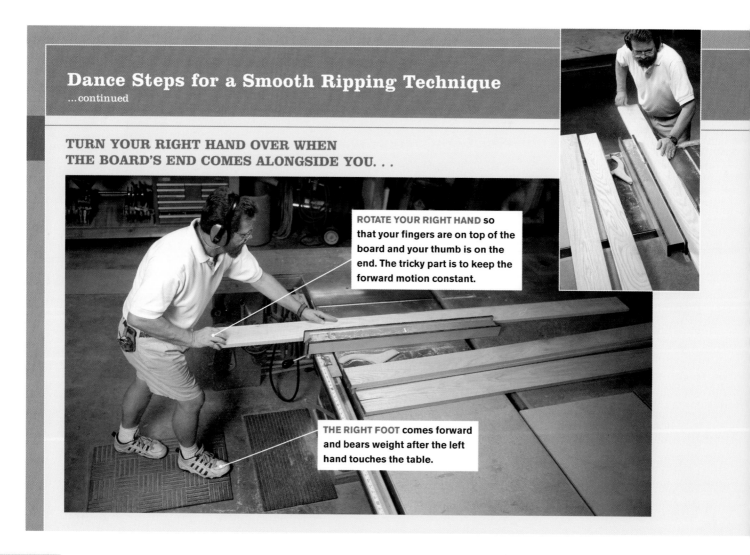

Dance Steps for a Smooth Ripping Technique
...continued

TURN YOUR RIGHT HAND OVER WHEN THE BOARD'S END COMES ALONGSIDE YOU. . .

ROTATE YOUR RIGHT HAND so that your fingers are on top of the board and your thumb is on the end. The tricky part is to keep the forward motion constant.

THE RIGHT FOOT comes forward and bears weight after the left hand touches the table.

Practice Makes Perfect

If this all sounds complicated, it is—at first. My suggestion for learning this technique is to practice. I recommend using an 8-ft. length of ¾-in. particleboard about 10 in. wide. Its weight and cutting resistance are similar to hardwood. Using particleboard keeps you from turning a lovely piece of cherry into kindling. The idea is to practice the hand and foot movements until the motion is entirely fluid.

Make several cuts in succession, taking off about ¼ in. with each cut, but never less than ³⁄₁₆ in. or just enough so the blade is fully engaged with the board. If the blade runs free, it will oscillate slightly. As it engages the wood, the kerf made in the wood dampens this oscillation. The design of a good blade takes this into account. If it is cutting only on one side—not fully engaged in the wood—a tablesaw blade will continue to oscillate and will produce a gouged edge.

For the learning session, use your utility tablesaw blade because particleboard is quite abrasive and will quickly dull a triple-chip blade. After a dozen or so cuts, the process should start to feel familiar and will become as natural a movement as any.

LON SCHLEINING is a woodworker in Dana Point, Calif. He is the author of *Treasure Chests* (2001) and *The Workbench* (2004), both published by The Taunton Press, Inc.

AND FINISH THE CUT WITH YOUR RIGHT HAND ONLY.

THE RIGHT HAND pushes the board all the way through the cut. To keep the board tight against the fence, use your thumb to exert a twisting action to the right on the end of the board.

Getting the First Edge Straight on a Tablesaw

The jointer is unmatched at making a warped board straight and flat on its face. It's what they were designed to do. However, they aren't the only machine that can get a first edge straight on an uneven board. For edge-jointing the S2S lumber I buy, I choose my tablesaw every time. I find it works faster. Where it might take 10 passes over a jointer to get a straight edge, I can do it on the first pass over my tablesaw with a minimum of setup.

Unlike the jointer, the tablesaw needs a guide to do this. A piece of ¾-in.-thick plywood for a template, slightly wider than the board to be cut,

and a few brads are all you need. Make sure the edges of the plywood are straight and parallel.

I align one edge of the plywood along the board exactly where I want the cut to take place so that the waste edge of the board is peeking out from under the plywood. I then nail the plywood to the top of the board with small brads. You usually only need one nail at each end, and by using a longer-than-needed board, you can cut off each end where the nails left holes.

I set the fence to the width of the plywood and guide the assembly through the saw as I would if it were a single board (see the photo at left). I keep the edge of the plywood against the rip fence and—just like magic—the edge of the board below is cut straight as a string pulled tight.

This technique can be used to straighten rough edges and crooked edges or to cut tapers.

EDGE-JOINTING WITHOUT A JOINTER. The template registers against the rip fence and guides uneven boards through a straight cut.

Safe Procedures at the Tablesaw

BY HOWARD LEWIN

A tablesaw doesn't have a conscience. It couldn't care less whether or not it cuts off your finger. And it will. If you know this going in, then you can guard against it. What I try to do is arm myself with knowledge of what the machine is likely to do and then stop it before it happens.

Kickback, the main cause of most tablesaw injuries, occurs when the board drifts away from the fence and pushes against the back of the spinning blade. As the teeth come out of the back side of the saw, they will actually lift the board off the table and launch it over the top of the blade. When that happens, the board is propelled with a few horsepower of force behind it.

Splitters are designed to prevent kickback, and they do. Yet they cause a great deal of anxiety to me and most of the woodworkers I know. This is probably because the splitters that are readily available in the United States aren't quite up to par. For a splitter to do its job, it has to be the exact width of the blade. If the splitter is narrower than the blade, then it allows room for the board to slide away from the fence. If it is thicker than the blade, it forces the stock into the front of the blade and jams the board.

European splitters, like those on Inca tablesaws, attach directly behind the blade and are curved to follow the blade's arc. The splitter adjusts and travels with the blade, allowing dado and bevel cuts. It is useful, and it works. The splitters on most American saws have to be removed to make these cuts. Often they are not replaced.

As for blade guards, they work fine, except when you really need them. When you are cutting plywood or long boards with wide dimensions, your hand is nowhere near the blade; therefore, it's pretty safe. It's when you have to do detail work close to the blade that you need a blade guard but can't use one.

Warning:

Fine Woodworking does not recommend the removal of splitters, blade guards, or other safety devices from tablesaws. The author of this article believes that many woodworkers choose to operate tablesaws without such devices. Our observations as editors confirm this. We also recognize that many woodworkers own older machines or used tablesaws that came without these safety mechanisms. In all these cases, it is essential that the safety steps outlined in the following article be taken to minimize the risk of injury.

PUSH STICKS, PUSH PADDLES, AND PUSH SHOES

Push sticks lend leverage when guiding stock through a cut. The notch allows you to hold the push stick at about a 45° angle and keeps your hand about 10 in. above the blade. Wider push sticks give a more solid connection. Just make sure the grain runs lengthwise, so it won't break when the notched end passes through the blade. Cut them in bulk, so there's always one nearby. On narrow stock, push shoes hold the stock flush to the tabletop and afford even more leverage. Push paddles offer the most control. If the lumber is heavy or wide, use push paddles to help ease the way past the blade.

THROW NO SPARKS. When you build a push paddle with dowels, you don't have to worry about the blade catching an errant screw. A layer of sandpaper over the paddle's face will help it grip the stock.

ZERO-CLEARANCE INSERTS

Zero-clearance inserts prevent the loss of thin strips in the wide clearance allowed by most factory inserts. They also prevent tearout by supporting the stock all the way up to the blade. First make a pattern from the factory cut insert, usually ½ in. thick, and then shape it to a press fit from the pattern. Drill a ¾-in. hole in the insert to serve as an easy finger pull. Change them when you have to switch blades or make beveled cuts.

Though splitters and blade guards should work better and should be more widely used, I see little use in pretending that they are.

What is imperative is that you take the necessary measures to ensure safety at the tablesaw. I always use zero-clearance tablesaw inserts, featherboards, and push sticks. I keep a well-tuned saw, and I let a few rules guide my work.

- Never stand directly behind the sawblade.
- Make sure the blade is never more than ⅛ in. above the board being cut.
- Be aware of what the wood is doing at all times. And be ready to react.
- Never back a board out of a cut.
- At the slightest hint that a board is bowing away from the fence, lift it out of the cut and above the blade. Then begin to make the cut again.

To drive a car you have to pass a test. The same is true for flying an airplane or sailing a boat. Most people even take the time to get some kind of computer training these days. But the same people simply take a tablesaw out of the box and cut away. It doesn't make much sense. If you make a mistake at the computer, what's the worst scenario—you loose a page, some book-keeping? But make a mistake at the table-saw, and the consequences are much greater. Digits don't grow back.

The photos and drawings on the following pages show the basic setups for safe cutting. With these things in mind, you can foresee problems and prevent them before they happen.

HOWARD LEWIN is a woodworker and woodworking teacher in Hawthorne, Calif.

FEATHERBOARDS

When clamped to the tablesaw, featherboards help the board ride the fence throughout the cut. Even if a board does wander from the fence, the feathered end helps prevent it from kicking back. They are easily made with scrap stock and a bandsaw. The angled end should be cut at 30° to 40° and the feathered kerfs bandsawn at about ¼-in. intervals. For larger stock, use wider and thicker featherboards. It's good to make them in various sizes so an appropriate one is always nearby.

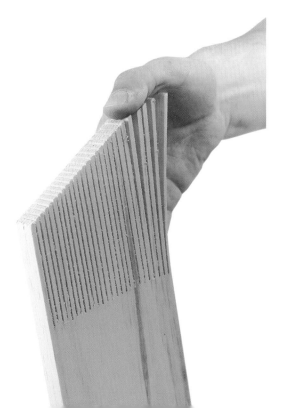

The safest and easiest way to crosscut is to use a sled. It enables you to keep your fingers at a safe distance from the blade. A smooth feed rate and a sharp, pitch-free blade with at least 30 teeth to 40 teeth should allow you to crosscut without a glitch. A crosscut sled can also be set up to cut angles and compound miters.

The sled has an additional box added to the back, so fingers won't get cut off in the blade's path.

The sled is as wide as the top of the saw. The wider the sled, the longer the stock the saw can easily handle.

The sled rests flush on the table. It is guided by rails that ride in the miter slots.

Routed slots on the outfeed table accommodate the sled's guide rails. The slots allow the sled to pass across the full length of the blade.

A scrap of wood clamped to the sled acts as a stop block. It allows you to cut numerous boards to uniform length.

CROSSCUTTING WITH A MITER GAUGE

You can also crosscut using a miter gauge with an extension fence screwed or clamped to it. The extension fence will support the board all the way up to the blade.

USING THE RIP FENCE AS A STOP

Clamp an extra piece of wood to the fence to act as a stop block. This prevents the wood from getting trapped between the fence and the blade, which can cause it to bind and kick back. Never use the fence alone to crosscut boards.

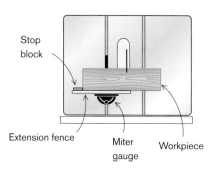

Stop block

Extension fence   Miter gauge   Workpiece

To cut a number of pieces to the same length, attach a stop block directly onto the extension fence.

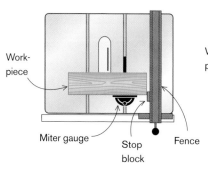

Workpiece

Miter gauge   Stop block   Fence

When possible, use the miter gauge between the fence and the blade.

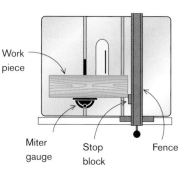

Work piece

Miter gauge   Stop block   Fence

For trimming smaller pieces to length, move the miter gauge to the left of the blade.

Ripping

Before ripping a board to size, make sure you have a perfectly flat side against the fence. Do not stop the cut or reduce pressure until you have pushed the material past the blade. If the board begins to drift from the blade or if the board moves in any way that makes you uncomfortable, lift it out of the cut and begin again. A sharp, clean blade goes a long way toward keeping procedures safe. For general ripping, 30 teeth to 40 teeth are adequate. For thicker stock—2 in. or more—use wider kerf blades with fewer teeth.

Always stand to the left of the blade, never directly behind the board you are cutting. This is the only way that you can exert the pressure necessary to keep the board against the fence. It also puts you in the best spot if the board does kick back.

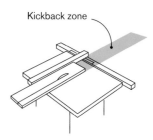

Kickback zone

KEEP TO THE FENCE

When pushing a board through a cut, always apply pressure on the side closest to the blade.

Right

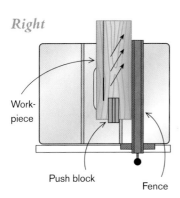

Workpiece

Push block

Fence

Wrong

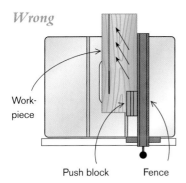

Workpiece

Push block

Fence

Extension tables help keep the boards flat on the table and lessen the chance that a board will wander as it moves past the blade.

Always use featherboards placed just in front of the blade to prevent kickback.

MANAGING BOWED STOCK

If you must rip or crosscut a board that is bowed or cupped, even slightly, place the board with the concave side facing down.

Right   *Wrong*

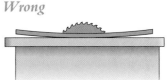

Beveling

O n right-tilting saws, cutting bevels traps the board between the fence and the blade, which should cause you great anxiety. You can avoid this problem by moving the fence to the left of the blade. Using zero-clearance inserts is the only way to ensure that small cutoffs don't get sucked into the saw.

RIPPING AT AN ANGLE

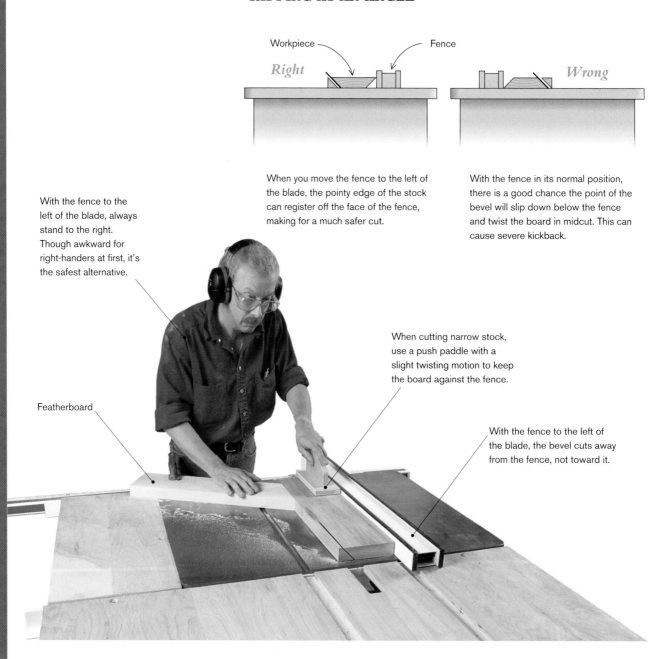

Workpiece — Fence

Right *Wrong*

When you move the fence to the left of the blade, the pointy edge of the stock can register off the face of the fence, making for a much safer cut.

With the fence in its normal position, there is a good chance the point of the bevel will slip down below the fence and twist the board in midcut. This can cause severe kickback.

With the fence to the left of the blade, always stand to the right. Though awkward for right-handers at first, it's the safest alternative.

Featherboard

When cutting narrow stock, use a push paddle with a slight twisting motion to keep the board against the fence.

With the fence to the left of the blade, the bevel cuts away from the fence, not toward it.

RAISING A PANEL

To make raised-panel cuts on a right-tilting tablesaw, you must move the fence to the left of the blade. This way, the blade is angled away from the fence. And you must use an auxiliary fence tall enough to allow a firm handhold on the piece being beveled. Because of the small offcuts you're creating, zero-clearance inserts are absolutely necessary.

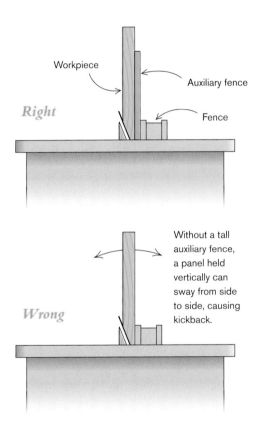

Right

Workpiece

Auxiliary fence

Fence

Wrong

Without a tall auxiliary fence, a panel held vertically can sway from side to side, causing kickback.

BEVELING WITH A LEFT-TILTING SAW

When you use a left-tilting saw, there is no need to move the fence to the less familiar left side of the saw. For beveled cuts, the blade is automatically angled away from the fence. For most, the result is a safer and much more comfortable procedure.

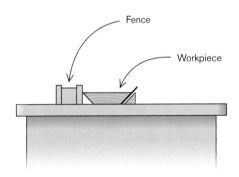

Fence

Workpiece

Needing a left-tilting arbor is probably not reason enough to buy a new saw, but if you're in the market and are right-handed, it's an option worth looking for. Powermatic and Craftsman have been making left-tilting saws for a number of years; and a few other manufacturers, Delta and Jet among them, have recently introduced these machines.

RABBETS

When cutting rabbets, an auxiliary fence clamped or screwed in place keeps the blade from digging into the primary fence. On wider stock, when there is more than 6 in. against the fence, a miter gauge is not required– simply run the edge of the board along the fence. You can also use a crosscut slide or a miter gauge to cut rabbets. And remember, never go backward across a blade.

GROOVES

To cut a groove on the edge of a board, an auxiliary fence and zero-clearance inserts are essential. Use a feather-board in front of the blade to hold the stock against the fence. On narrower boards, be sure to use a push stick, and apply downward pressure through and past the blade. Cut the groove as close to the fence as possible.

DADOES

Always dado as close to the fence as possible. Narrow stock requires a miter gauge and a stop block. On wider stock, where there is more than 6 in. against the fence and less than a 4-in. gap between the blade and the fence, a miter gauge is not required. Never dado far from the fence even with a miter gauge. You can also use a crosscut sled dedicated to making dado cuts.

Taming Tearout on the Tablesaw

One major factor that separates a good piece of furniture from a mediocre one is how cleanly it is constructed. Nothing will kill the look of a finished piece more than tearout. Those rough edges are inexcusable and can be avoided if you pay attention to how wood fibers react to different types of tooling.

Most tearout on the tablesaw occurs when the blade exits the stock and breaks the wood fibers rather than cutting them. As a result, splinters may show up on the underside, back corner, and back edge of a workpiece. This is especially relevant to crosscutting on the tablesaw. But tearout is not hard to eliminate or manage. The first item to look at is the sawblade.

The Correct Blade Is the First Line of Defense

It is important that the blade is designated for the type of cut being performed and that it's sharp and clean; a dull blade, or one covered with pitch, will produce a poor-quality cut. Crosscutting blades and many general-purpose blades have teeth with alternating bevels. The staggered teeth on these blades are beneficial because they score the fibers before hogging out the stock.

Avoid trim cuts Sometimes tearout occurs by taking too light of a trim cut. It often is better to have material on both sides of the blade; that way, the wood fibers are supported across the full width of the kerf and onto the offcut. This tension keeps the fibers from ripping away. On trim cuts, the fibers are more inclined to break away, which can be a real problem when working with manufactured panel products, such as plywood, and with porous woods, such as oak.

Raise the blade to reduce tearout The height of the tablesaw blade also is an issue, although a controversial one. The rules of safety declare that the blade should project above the surface about the height of a

BY STEVE LATTA

Shop Aids Prevent Tearout

Tearout mostly occurs on a crosscut when the sawblade breaks the wood fibers rather than splitting them. Once you understand the common causes of tearout, you can follow a few simple guidelines to prevent it.

Identify Trouble Spots

Tearout is most likely to occur on the underside of the workpiece as well as on the back edge and back corners (below and top left). A wide kerf in the tablesaw insert or crosscut sled also can allow tearout (bottom left and right).

The back edge and bottom surface of the workpiece are prone to tearout.

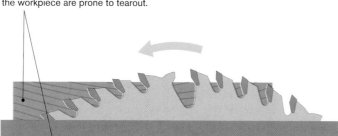

Install a Zero-Clearance Insert

A zero-clearance insert increases the support area under the workpiece and reduces the chance of tearout.

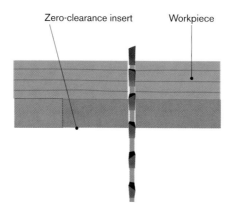

Zero-clearance insert   Workpiece

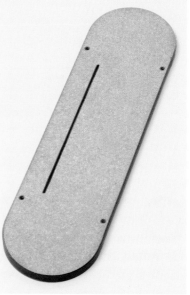

Inserts may be bought or shopmade. Several manufacturers make aftermarket inserts that replace the one that came with your saw. A wood insert also can be made in the shop.

Use a Crosscut Sled

Another solution is to use a crosscut sled. If the original kerf has become too wide, add a fresh auxiliary deck and fence and make zero-clearance kerfs in them.

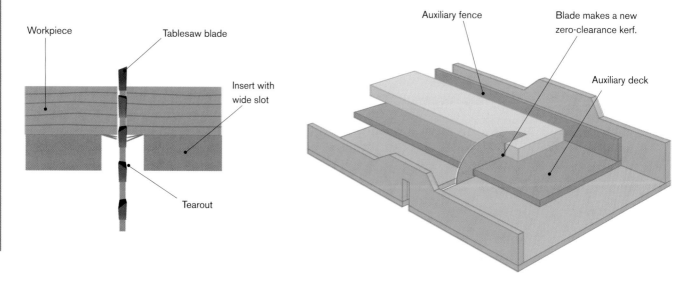

Workpiece   Tablesaw blade

Insert with wide slot

Tearout

Auxiliary fence

Blade makes a new zero-clearance kerf.

Auxiliary deck

Orient the Workpiece to Hide Tearout

1. TABLE LEGS

IDENTIFY THE INSIDE EDGES OF TABLE LEGS. With the legs oriented with the exposed faces outward, mark the unexposed sides of the legs with a crayon.

PLACE THE HIDDEN SIDES OF THE LEG AGAINST THE FENCE AND DECK. Orient the leg on the tablesaw so that the blade exits the workpiece on a surface that won't be visible on the finished furniture piece.

2. DRAWER FRONTS

ORIENT DRAWER FRONTS SO THAT TEAROUT IS RESTRICTED TO THE INSIDE FACE. Crosscut drawer fronts with the exposed face up.

ROTATE, DON'T FLIP THE DRAWER FACE. When crosscutting the other end of a drawer front, make sure the exposed face is still on top.

Order Your Cuts to Eliminate Tearout

WHICH COMES FIRST, THE DADO OR THE RABBET? The dado comes first, if you follow the general rule that end-grain cuts should be made before long-grain cuts.

A RABBET WILL SCOOP AWAY TEAROUT CAUSED BY THE DADO CUT. Cut the rabbet deeper than the dado to ensure a clean edge.

A zero-clearance insert ensures that the workpiece is fully supported as it passes across the blade, thus reducing tearout (see p. 46). I've applied this same concept to my crosscutting sled, which has developed a wide kerf from use. Each time I use a sled for a new operation, I affix an auxiliary deck and fence on which a workpiece will rest as it is run through the saw. Once I've applied the fresh deck and fence, I run it through the saw and produce a new kerf that is the exact width of the blade. Now the new kerf also serves as a reference point for lining up successive cuts.

Isolate Tearout to Hidden Surfaces

In my woodworking courses, nothing knocks down a student's grade faster than visible tearout on a finished piece. I've often seen this occur on the top of a table leg as a result of the student improperly cutting it to length.

You should have a good idea how the legs will be positioned on a table before you make any cuts. As noted earlier, the bottom face, back corner, and back edge of a workpiece are most susceptible to tearout. Thus, table legs should be oriented on the saw so the outside faces of the leg make first contact with the blade. This way, any tearout won't be visible once the table has been assembled. I always mark the inside faces and end grain of a leg before cutting it to length to remind me of the proper orientation. This same concept can be applied to a cut on the miter saw, which will produce tearout in a similar fashion.

Another example of properly orienting a workpiece to limit tearout is when trimming a drawer front to length. The piece should be positioned with its inside face against the tabletop so tearout is isolated to the unseen face. After making the first cut, rotate the stock and cut the other end, don't flip it. Rotating the stock places all of the tearout on the back face; flipping it will result in tearout on the inside and outside faces.

tooth. Regretfully, a low blade height can lift fibers away from the surface, especially toward the end of the cut.

Raising the blade higher than normally recommended transfers the forces of blade rotation in such a manner that the fibers are pressed into the surface, resulting in a cleaner cut. In many applications, I raise the blade at least 1 in. above the workpiece and take extra precautions to ensure safety.

Use a Zero-Clearance Insert or Crosscut Sled

Another common cause of tearout when crosscutting is a tablesaw insert in which the blade slot is too wide—typical on most stock inserts. This slot is a hot zone for tearout because it creates an unsupported surface for the material being cut. The hard edge where the workpiece finally becomes supported serves as a chipbreaker and allows the fibers to tear as far as the hard edge.

Score or Tape the Workpiece Before Cutting

TAPE TROUBLESOME AREAS. The unsupported corners on this workpiece will tear when crosscut on the tablesaw if preventive measures aren't taken.

SCORE THE CUTLINE. When crosscutting a cabinet door to length, score a line around the underside and back edge of the cross-grain stile to reduce the chances of tearout on those trouble spots.

Cut End Grain Before Cutting Long Grain

The proper sequencing of cuts also plays a vital role in how clean a project will turn out. In general, when a workpiece needs to be cut across the grain and along the grain, it's best to cut the end grain first. This old standby holds true for most machining processes, from raising panels to rabbeting drawer bottoms. If tearout does occur from the blade (or cutter) exiting the end grain, the long-grain pass will scoop away any blowout that might have occurred.

There are a number of operations where this rule holds true. One good example is a bookcase that uses dadoes to fix shelves and a rabbet to hold the back boards. Which comes first—the dado or the rabbet? If we follow the rule of end grain first, the dado would need to come first. Rabbeting the back afterward removes any tearout produced along the back end of the dado.

Scoring and Taping Can Help Reduce Tearout

Due diligence also will prevent tearout. For example, when working on large cabinet projects, I always make frame-and-panel

doors slightly oversize, then cut them to fit once I can determine the exact dimensions of the opening that the door will fill. However, when cutting a door to height, you encroach on a major problem area: the back edge on the door stile where the sawblade is cutting end grain.

Using a marking knife or an X-Acto® knife, I score a line on the bottom side and back edge of the stile where it will be cut on the tablesaw. This scored line will allow the fibers to break cleanly before they have a chance to tear out.

Applying clear tape to an edge that is to be cut also works well to prevent tearout, but special care has to be taken when pulling off the tape. Peeling it off in the direction of the fibers will lay them down. If you peel it off in the other direction, the tape will lift the fibers. Sometimes a very light film of white glue rubbed over a troublesome area will provide enough support to keep fibers from tearing. Just make sure that all of the glue is removed before it comes time to apply a finish.

STEVE LATTA is an instructor at the Thaddeus Stevens College of Technology in Lancaster, Penn.

Cutting Coves on the Tablesaw

BY STUART SABOL

Coves often are used as a decorative element in the design of furniture and architectural moldings. Whether in the feet of a chest, in a transition section between upper and lower cases, or in crown molding, coves create delicate shadow lines that accent and enhance a workpiece.

There are two broad categories of coves: symmetrical and asymmetrical. A symmetrical cove has its apex (highest point) in the center. The apex of an asymmetrical cove is offset from the center (see the photos and drawings on the facing page).

Large professional shops cut coves on a shaper, but few amateurs can justify the expense of one of these industrial machines. The alternative method is to cut coves on a tablesaw; no expensive attachments are needed, and an infinite variety of coves is possible. The drawback, however, is that it can be difficult to set up the tablesaw to cut coves to precise shapes.

I use two methods that simplify the tablesaw setup: The first involves the use of a simple shopmade parallelogram for cutting symmetrical coves; the second uses a computer spreadsheet program to establish the correct angles when cutting the more complicated asymmetrical coves.

Symmetrical Coves Are Cut with the Blade at 90°

A cove has two defining dimensions: the depth of the cut that equals the height of the blade above the table, and the width of the cove measured at its base (see the drawing on p. 52). These two dimensions

The waist and crown moldings on this cabinet were made on the table-saw by feeding the stock across the blade at an angle. The symmetrical waist molding was cut with the sawblade perpendicular to the tablesaw top. The elongated crown molding was created by tilting the sawblade.

SYMMETRICAL An upright blade produces a cove that has its apex at the center.

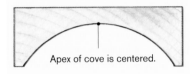

Apex of cove is centered.

ASYMMETRICAL A tilted blade produces a cove with an off-center apex.

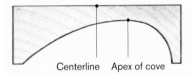

Centerline   Apex of cove

are varied by adjusting the height of the sawblade and by varying the angle at which the workpiece approaches the sawblade. Make a scaled drawing of the design or use a scaled plan, and measure the depth of the cove and the width at the base.

Use a shopmade parallelogram to set up the cuts The parallelogram makes it easy to determine the fence angle for a symmetrical cove. The parallelogram is roughly 1 ft. by 2 ft. and is made from any straight-edged scraps of wood. Join the pieces with machine screws and wing nuts, and countersink the heads of the screws so that the parallelogram can lie flat on the saw table.

Raise the sawblade to match the depth of the cove. Measure the width of the cove, and set the inside gap between the long sides of the parallelogram to match it. Lay the parallelogram on the tablesaw so that it straddles the blade. Rotate the parallelogram until the front tooth of the saw is just touching the front of the parallelogram and the back tooth is just touching the back (see the drawing on p. 53). Mark the front inside edge of the parallelogram. Set the miter gauge to this angle, and use it to determine the angle of the fence. Before clamping the fence to the saw table, allow for the offset of the cove from the edge of the workpiece. The offset is measured perpendicular from the fence to the closest blade tooth.

Symmetrical coves can be cut with one fence. It should be at least ¾ in. thick, 3 in. wide, and 3 ft. to 4 ft. long, jointed on two adjacent edges. (If it is difficult to set a clamp on the front rail, clamp braces to an extension table, as shown on p. 55.) If your design leaves the workpiece thin above the apex of the cove, add a second fence behind the sawblade to support the workpiece as you bear down on it. The rear fence also lessens the chance of the wood splitting along the line of the apex.

Lower the blade to just below the table, noting how many turns of the handle this takes; as a backup, mark the final depth of the cove on the end of the workpiece.

Make a dry run to practice the feed rate, to make sure the fence gives adequate guidance, and to check that none of the clamps is an obstruction.

Cut in small bites, and feed slowly The cut is made by passing the workpiece at an angle over the blade rather than straight into the cutting edge. This means that the blade teeth are in contact over the full arc of the cove and remove a considerable amount of wood; therefore, a cove must be cut in small increments, no more than about ⅛ in. at a time. Also, you need to employ a slow feed rate because the thrust is against the side of the blade—a cut for which the blade is not designed. For a deep cove, each pass should remove less and less

Making a Symmetrical Cove

START WITH A FULL-SIZE DRAWING

To set up the tablesaw for cutting a cove, first make a full-size drawing of the desired cove. To vary the depth and width of a cove, adjust the height of the blade and the angle at which the workpiece approaches it. The cove's offset is determined by the distance between the fence and the sawblade.

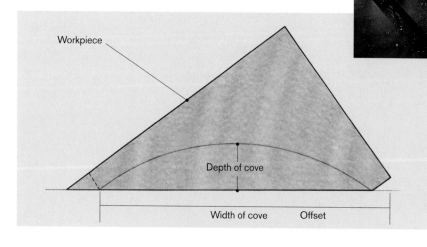

SETTING THE BLADE HEIGHT FOR A SYMMETRICAL COVE. **Raise the blade to match the depth of the cove. The blade is lowered after the setup to cut in ⅛-in. increments.**

Workpiece

Depth of cove

Width of cove   Offset

material because the arc length increases, requiring more power from the saw to make the cut.

To cut coves safely on the tablesaw, be sure to use push sticks or, better yet, a pair of padded push blocks like those normally used with a jointer.

When you've almost reached the cove's final depth, make a very shallow cut to leave the surface of the cove as smooth as possible. You also can make a second pass with the blade at the final height to further reduce the amount of scraping and sanding.

Asymmetrical Coves Are Cut with the Blade Tilted

As the sun sets, an object's shadow becomes elongated; circles become ovals, stretching until almost losing their curvature just before night falls. In a similar way, tilting the blade distorts and elongates a cove. As the angles of the blade and the auxiliary fence become more oblique, the apex of the blade is moved to a point away from the cove centerline.

While you can use the parallelogram to measure the angle of approach, it cannot reveal the shape of the cove if the blade is tilted. The traditional method has been to sight across the blade and experiment with blade and fence angles until the profile of the blade matches that of the cove. This method requires repeated trial cuts with scrapwood. A better approach is to use a spreadsheet program to calculate the blade and fence angles (see p. 56). The spreadsheet

USE A PARALLELOGRAM TO DETERMINE THE FENCE ANGLE

The shopmade parallelogram (about 1 ft. by 2 ft.) is made from scraps of wood, joined with machine screws and wing nuts. The screws are countersunk so that the parallelogram can lie flat.

SETTING THE WIDTH. **Adjust the parallelogram to match the width of the cove. Then place it on the tablesaw and rotate it until the teeth at table level just touch both sides.**

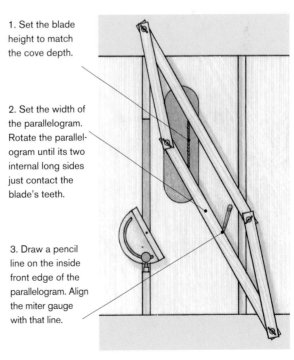

1. Set the blade height to match the cove depth.

2. Set the width of the parallelogram. Rotate the parallelogram until its two internal long sides just contact the blade's teeth.

3. Draw a pencil line on the inside front edge of the parallelogram. Align the miter gauge with that line.

program also can be used to find the fence angle to cut symmetrical coves.

As with a symmetrical cove, an asymmetrical cove starts with a scale drawing. Measure the cove's depth, length, and apex offset. Enter the data in the spreadsheet. Start with your tablesaw's blade diameter; then enter the desired depth of the cove, the desired length of the cove, and the length of the apex offset. Enter 0 or 90, according to the midpoint setting on your miter gauge. Then click on the Calculate button, and the spreadsheet will show you the correct angle to tilt your sawblade and the correct angle to align your auxiliary fence.

The spreadsheet also displays the exact cove length and apex offset these blade and fence angles will produce. They should be almost identical to your desired dimensions.

Use extra caution when cutting asymmetrical coves It's important to use two fences to cut asymmetrical coves: one in the front and one in the rear. The extra fence will allow you to apply more downward force and will keep the workpiece aligned over the blade.

When cutting symmetrical coves with the blade vertical, it is safe to feed the work

Making a Symmetrical Cove continued

LOCATE AND SECURE THE FENCE

Rest the fence against the miter gauge and measure any offset required. The fence should be at least ¾ in. thick by 3 in. wide and jointed on two adjacent sides. Clamp both ends of the fence to the tablesaw. Add braces, if necessary, for additional support.

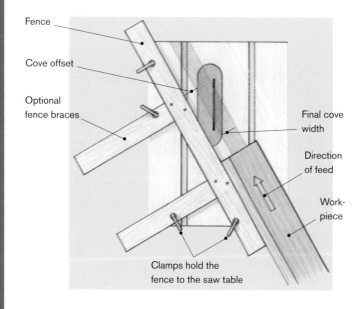

Fence

Cove offset

Optional fence braces

Final cove width

Direction of feed

Work-piece

Clamps hold the fence to the saw table

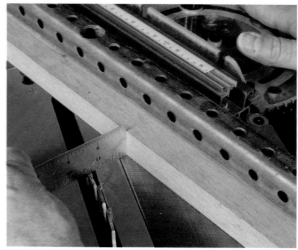

SET THE OFFSET. If the cove does not reach the edge of the workpiece, this gap, known as the offset, must be allowed for when setting the fence. The distance is perpendicular from the fence to the edge of the front sawtooth.

from either side of the blade. With asymmetrical coves, the blade is tilted, and you must feed the work from the side the blade is tilted toward. If you try to feed the work in the same direction the blade is tilting, there is a risk of the work sliding up the tilting blade, rising above the level of the front fence, and being thrown back at you. For a left-tilting saw, feed from the left front; for a right-tilting saw, feed from the right front.

Once the feed direction has been determined, set up the auxiliary fence in the correct orientation (see the drawings on pp. 56–57). The apex will be offset from the centerline of the cove in a direction opposite from where you feed the workpiece. Feeding into the blade from the front of the table moves the apex to the back of the workpiece. Lay out the asymmetrical cove on the workpiece so that it will blend with any other decorative elements, and orient

CLAMP THE FENCE. Once the fence angle and the offset distance have been set, clamp the fence securely to the table. If it is difficult to set a clamp on the front rail, use braces clamped to the extension table.

APPLY STEADY PRESSURE AND TAKE SMALL BITES. Because the workpiece is being pushed across the blade and not through it, the blade should be raised by only ⅛ in. for each pass. Push down and toward the fence with a large padded push block, such as this tile-grout trowel, and forward with a push stick.

TABLESAW COVES NEED CLEANING UP

However slow the final pass, some saw marks will remain. The two best ways to achieve a smooth surface are either to use a gooseneck scraper, which has a variable profile that should fit any cove, or to sand the surface.

SHOPMADE PROFILE SANDER. Transfer the shape of the cove onto some building foam (left) and then cut the foam to shape on a bandsaw. With sandpaper wrapped around the custom-shaped foam block (right), sanding the cove goes smoothly.

SCRAPE AWAY SAW MARKS A gooseneck scraper should fit any cove profile. Turn an edge on the scraper with the burnisher.

Making an Asymmetrical Cove

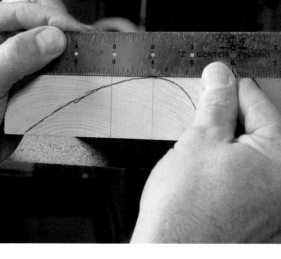

THE AMOUNT OF BLADE TILT WILL DETERMINE THE COVE SHAPE

As the blade is tilted toward 45°, the shape of the cove becomes increasingly asymmetrical, with the apex of the cove farther and farther away from the centerline of the workpiece.

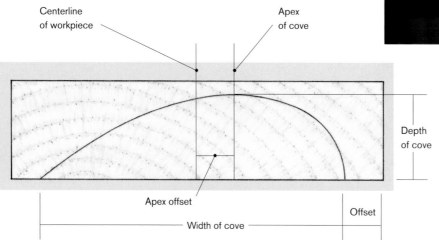

Centerline of workpiece

Apex of cove

Depth of cove

Apex offset

Offset

Width of cove

THIS COVE HAS THREE DIMEN-SIONS. Record the width and depth of the cove, and measure the distance between the centerline of the workpiece and the apex of the cove; in this case, it's just over 1 in.

Use a Computer Spreadsheet to Establish Blade-Tilt and Fence Angles

My spreadsheet will help you calculate the proper blade and fence angles to cut coves on the tablesaw. Enter data only in the five squares in the center of the spreadsheet. Simply enter the diameter of your sawblade, the desired cove depth, length, and apex offset, hit Calculate, and the spreadsheet will calculate the correct angle to tilt the sawblade and to set the auxiliary fence. If your cove dimensions fall outside the limitations of your tablesaw, the spreadsheet also will show you the maximum possible dimensions. You can customize the spreadsheet for your miter gauge by entering 90 or 0, depending on your gauge's midpoint setting. You also can use the spreadsheet for symmetrical coves by entering 0 for the apex offset, which eliminates the value for the blade-tilt angle.

COMPUTER HELP. Sabol's spreadsheet program determines the correct fence and blade angles. It also will tell you if the dimensions of the cove are beyond the capabilities of your tablesaw.

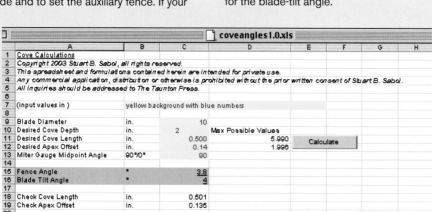

coveangles1.0.xls

	A	B	C	D	E	F	G	H
1	Cove Calculations							
2	Copyright 2003 Stuart B. Sabol, all rights reserved.							
3	This spreadsheet and formulations contained herein are intended for private use.							
4	Any commercial application, distribution or otherwise is prohibited without the prior written consent of Stuart B. Sabol.							
5	All inquiries should be addressed to The Taunton Press.							
6								
7	(input values in)	yellow background with blue numbers						
8								
9	Blade Diameter	in.	10					
10	Desired Cove Depth	in.	2	Max Possible Values				
11	Desired Cove Length	in.	0.500		5.990			
12	Desired Apex Offset	in.	0.14		1.996	Calculate		
13	Miter Gauge Midpoint Angle	90°/0°	90					
14								
15	Fence Angle	°	3.8					
16	Blade Tilt Angle	°	4					
17								
18	Check Cove Length	in.	0.501					
19	Check Apex Offset	in.	0.135					
20								

BLADE-TILT DIRECTION DETERMINES THE FEED DIRECTION

The correct feed direction will prevent the workpiece from riding up the tilted blade.
For a left-tilting blade, feed from the left; for a right-tilting blade, feed from the right.

Left-Tilting Saw

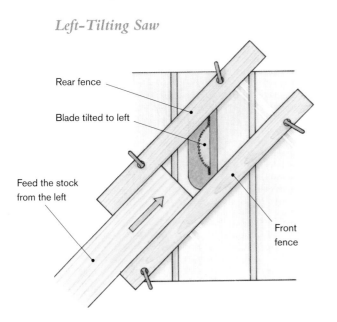

Rear fence

Blade tilted to left

Feed the stock
from the left

Front
fence

Right-Tilting Saw

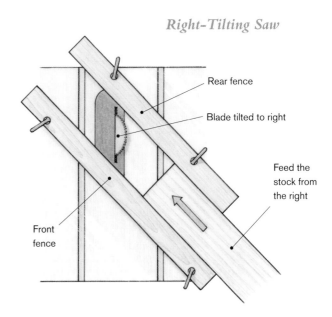

Rear fence

Blade tilted to right

Feed the
stock from
the right

Front
fence

FEED INTO THE TILTING BLADE. The workpiece should approach from the side that the blade is tilting toward. Otherwise, there is a risk that the workpiece may slide up the sloping blade and over the front fence.

DEEP COVES REQUIRE TWO FENCES

If the design leaves the workpiece thin above the apex of the cove, it is a good idea to add a second fence. Like the buttress of a bridge, this fence supports the workpiece as you bear down on it and lessens the chance of the wood splitting.

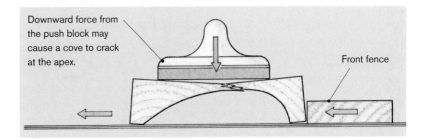

Downward force from
the push block may
cause a cove to crack
at the apex.

Front fence

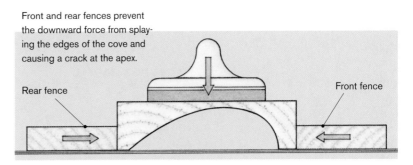

Front and rear fences prevent
the downward force from splaying the edges of the cove and
causing a crack at the apex.

Rear fence

Front fence

Coving with Different Miter Gauges

There are two main variations in the graduations of a miter gauge: The first is the number of degrees that the fence of the gauge can swing through. Most gauges that come with a tablesaw can move through 120°, but some are restricted to 90°. Many aftermarket gauges can swing through 180°, making them ideal for this process. Instead of buying another gauge, a simple solution is to cut a wedge that, when placed in front of the gauge, extends the angle range. Thus, if your gauge travels only 60° each side, a 30° wedge will extend that range to 90°.

The second variation is the different numbering methods of miter gauges. On some gauges, the midpoint is 90°, with the numbering system extending to 30° on each side. On other gauges, the midpoint is at 0°, and the numbers extend to 60° on both sides. The spreadsheet program (see p. 56) will work with both types of miter gauges.

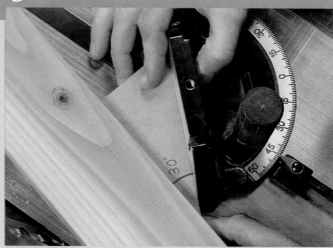

EXTEND THE RANGE OF ANGLES. If your miter gauge has a limited range, cut a wedge, subtract that angle from the desired angle, and set the miter gauge to that angle. In this case, 75° is obtained by using a 30° wedge and setting the angle at 45°.

the board so that the apex is translated in the proper direction before starting your passes over the blade.

Tablesawn Coves Have Limitations

The maximum cove length that can be cut on the tablesaw is directly related to the diameter of the blade and its cutting depth, and this relationship cannot be changed. You will be able to lengthen a cove with the same depth by tilting the blade and making an asymmetrical cove, but this technique reaches its limit rather quickly.

If a cove with a shallow cut and a long sweeping shape is desired, another method to shape the cove may be required, such as multiple cuts with a router and extensive cleanup.

In addition, narrow coves appear less circular and more elliptical, perhaps distracting from the initial intent of the designer. For narrow coves, using a smaller diameter blade can produce a cove with a more circular shape.

STUART SABOL is an engineer and amateur woodworker who lives in Houston, Tex.

Pattern Cutting on the Tablesaw

BY STEVE LATTA

When you mention pattern cutting to most woodworkers, they think of routers or shapers with bearing-guided cutters. But there are times when a tablesaw can be used just as effectively as a pattern-cutting tool, especially when the parts don't involve curves. Tablesaw pattern cutting is a great way to cut oddly shaped pieces or trim a door for an exact fit to a case. I pattern-cut parts large and small, square or with multiple angles, stuff that you just wouldn't normally cut on a tablesaw unless it was outfitted with a good, adjustable sliding table. The six-sided shelves of a corner cabinet are a prime example of what I'm talking about. Pattern cutting makes short work of these oddballs and leaves a cleanly machined and consistent product.

I know what you're thinking: This does not sound safe and sane. But because only a minimal amount of material is removed and an auxiliary fence covers the blade, this technique is no more dangerous than many tablesaw procedures. For my buck, I think it is safer than using a router table. A tablesaw is built for supporting large stock. Most router tables tend to scoot around when you lean on them.

The Template Serves Two Purposes

All pattern cutting involves the use of a template and a guide. In this method, a full-size pattern is used for the template, and a shopmade auxiliary fence acts as the guide. Use ¾-in.-thick stock—medium-density fiberboard (MDF), poplar, whatever's available—for the parts.

An Auxiliary Fence Guides the Template

The auxiliary fence is clamped to the saw's rip fence and serves as both a guide and guard. The workpiece, held by a template, slips under the fence and is trimmed by the sawblade. A cutout lets you see whether offcuts are collecting under the fence. Remove them only after the sawblade has stopped spinning.

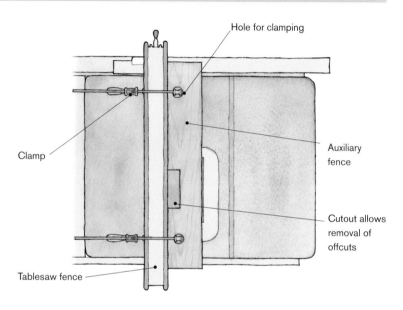

Hole for clamping

Clamp

Auxiliary fence

Cutout allows removal of offcuts

Tablesaw fence

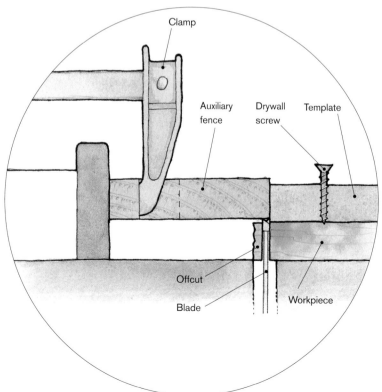

Clamp

Auxiliary fence

Drywall screw

Template

Offcut

Blade

Workpiece

A PIECE OF SCRAP IS USED TO SET THE FENCE HEIGHT. **The auxiliary fence should be ⅛ in. above the workpiece.**

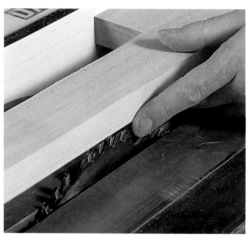

ALIGN THE FENCE FLUSH WITH THE SAWBLADE. **Make sure the teeth do not protrude beyond the edge of the fence.**

The fence consists of a piece of stock roughly ¾ in. thick by 5 in. wide by 24 in. long. Make a cutout so that you can keep an eye out for debris building up under the fence, and drill two large holes for clamping points. Clamp the auxiliary fence to the saw's rip fence about ⅛ in. or so higher than the workpiece. (The workpiece should slide freely beneath it.) Then move the entire fence assembly so that the auxiliary fence is flush with the outside teeth of the blade. Turn on the saw, and slowly raise the spinning blade until the teeth are cutting slightly into the underside of the auxiliary fence.

MDF is Ideal for Pattern Stock

For parts like a corner-cabinet shelf, a full-size fixed pattern makes the most sense. Begin by laying out the dimensions on a piece of ¾-in.-thick MDF. Next, rough-cut the pattern on the bandsaw, staying about ¹⁄₁₆ in. off the line. Then make a long MDF push stick, which will double as a guide for making the tablesaw cut. The push stick is long and wide enough to grip the workpiece safely. Attach sandpaper to the underside to get a good grip on the workpiece.

Creating a Pattern

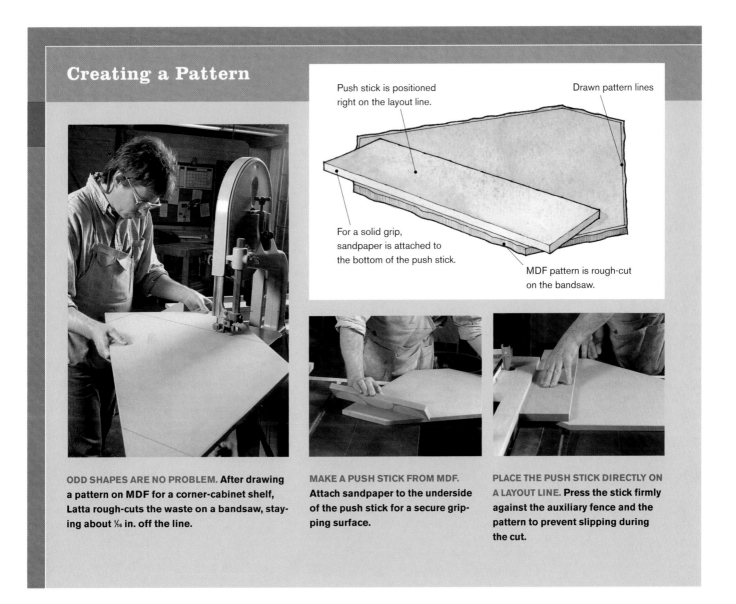

Push stick is positioned right on the layout line.

Drawn pattern lines

For a solid grip, sandpaper is attached to the bottom of the push stick.

MDF pattern is rough-cut on the bandsaw.

ODD SHAPES ARE NO PROBLEM. After drawing a pattern on MDF for a corner-cabinet shelf, Latta rough-cuts the waste on a bandsaw, staying about ¹⁄₁₆ in. off the line.

MAKE A PUSH STICK FROM MDF. Attach sandpaper to the underside of the push stick for a secure gripping surface.

PLACE THE PUSH STICK DIRECTLY ON A LAYOUT LINE. Press the stick firmly against the auxiliary fence and the pattern to prevent slipping during the cut.

You could also use screws; just keep them away from the cut line.

Place the push stick directly on a layout line of the pattern, then make the cut by running the push stick against the auxiliary fence. Push the stock through the blade, maintaining firm downward pressure. Because you've left only ¹⁄₁₆ in. of material on the pattern, the offcuts will be stringy pieces of stock that won't kick back. Those stringy parts may collect in a mass under the auxiliary fence, so periodically check the cutout for accumulation. If a buildup occurs, turn off the saw and remove the material with a stick or a blast of compressed air. Once the pattern has been cut, check it for accuracy. Fine adjustments can be made with a handplane.

Use the pattern to trace the shape onto the workpiece. Then rough-cut the workpiece on the bandsaw, staying a heavy ¹⁄₁₆ in. off the line. Before using the pattern, apply some sandpaper to the bottom side or drive some screws through it until the points just protrude and provide a solid grip on the workpiece. Place the pattern on the workpiece, and make the final cuts on the tablesaw. If everything has been set up properly, the pieces should be clean and identical.

THE PATTERN HAS TWO PURPOSES. Trace the shape onto the workpiece for rough cutting on the bandsaw. Then use it as a template for final trimming on the tablesaw.

Pattern Cutting Is a Great Way to Trim Doors to Fit a Case

When sizing doors to fit large cases, I make an adjustable jig that allows me to fine-tune individual doors to the case opening. On large cases, openings can shift a tad out of square, and this jig is especially handy if a case opening is slightly off. The jig consists of a piece of MDF with two adjustable pieces of hardwood mounted on each with battens. The combined assembly should be about ¾ in. shorter than the height of the opening. The adjustable hardwood sections should be slightly narrower than the main section so that they won't interfere with the case opening when making adjustments.

Place the jig into the door opening and place shims to account for the door gap above and below the jig. I use a couple of pieces of Formica® (you can get free sample squares at most home centers). With the MDF body of the jig held tightly against the case frame member that will receive the hinges, adjust the upper and lower portions of the jig with a screwdriver until you get a snug fit.

Lay the jig atop an assembled door, which you've built slightly larger than the case opening. Place the jig flush with the hinge stile, and position it so that the same amount of material will be removed from the top and bottom rails. With a sharp pencil, trace along the outside of the door frame using the jig as a guide. Score the edges and undersides of the stiles with a knife to avoid tearout.

Don't use the jig as a cutting guide. Instead, use an MDF push stick with sandpaper on the underside. Lay the push stick directly on a layout line, and make a cut by guiding the push stick along the edge of the auxiliary fence. Cut the door top and bottom this way. With any luck, you should have a great fit. A scraper and a little sandpaper will remove the saw marks on the top

Fitting Doors

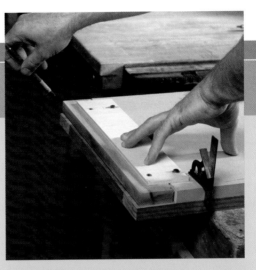

USE THE JIG AS A TRACING GUIDE. Line it up flush with one stile of the door, and mark the area to be trimmed.

LATTA USES AN ADJUSTABLE JIG TO SIZE DOORS. Shims above and below determine the gap. Slotted screw holes on the battens of the jig allow it to be adjusted for height and angle if the case is slightly out of square.

LAY A PUSH STICK DIRECTLY ON A LAY-OUT MARK. Cut each side of the door using the same method. Sandpaper on the underside of the push stick provides a secure grip. Do not use the adjustable jig for this process.

and bottom. After hinging the door, plane the far stile until you have a good fit.

Double doors are a little trickier only because the rails of both doors must match in width. After fitting the first door, take care to position the jig on the second door in such a way that you end up with rails of equal width. The eye will easily spot the unbalanced look of adjoining doors with mismatched rails. After hanging both doors, plane the center stiles for a consistent gap.

Once you understand this technique, you will find other uses for tablesaw pattern cutting. Just remember to rough-cut the workpiece on the bandsaw first, leaving only a small amount of material to remove on the tablesaw.

STEVE LATTA is an instructor at the Thaddeus Stevens College of Technology in Lancaster, Penn., and a member of the Executive Council for The Society of American Period Furniture Makers.

Box Joints on the Tablesaw

BY LON SCHLEINING

Boxes of every imaginable size and material can be assembled with mechanically interlocking box joints that are nearly as strong as the material itself. Box joints are not only reliable and attractive but also can be easy to make. They can be cut by hand or with a router, but I prefer to use a simple jig that fits onto my tablesaw crosscut sled. With this easily made accessory, you'll be able to assemble a strong, useful box in as little as an hour.

The same basic jig can be adapted to cut box joints as narrow as ⅛ in. or as wide as ¾ in., but I'll concentrate on ½-in.-wide joints—a useful size for drawer boxes and small chests.

Adapting a Crosscut Sled

My crosscut sled is easily the most useful and frequently used jig in my shop. If you have one already, great. If not, you'll soon wonder how you ever got along without one. As long as the sled is accurately made and works smoothly, it can be modified to cut box joints.

The rear fence must be substantial, because it will provide a mounting surface for the box-joint jig. To support the jig adequately, the rear fence on your crosscut sled must be secure, at least 5 in. or 6 in. high and square to the sled.

For ½-in. box joints, the sled will wind up with a ½-in. slot in it, but I'll also show you how to make a plywood insert that will return your sled to its more common uses, making it as good as new.

Setting up the Box-Joint Jig

I cut box joints no wider than the thickness of the material. The jig shown on the facing page is for cutting ½-in. joints, because it's a common and useful size. But ½ in. is only a

The Basic Box-Joint Jig

Adding a box-joint jig to a crosscut sled takes only a few bolts and scraps of plywood. This jig is set up to cut ½-in. joints, but the same methods can be used to make jigs for any joint size.

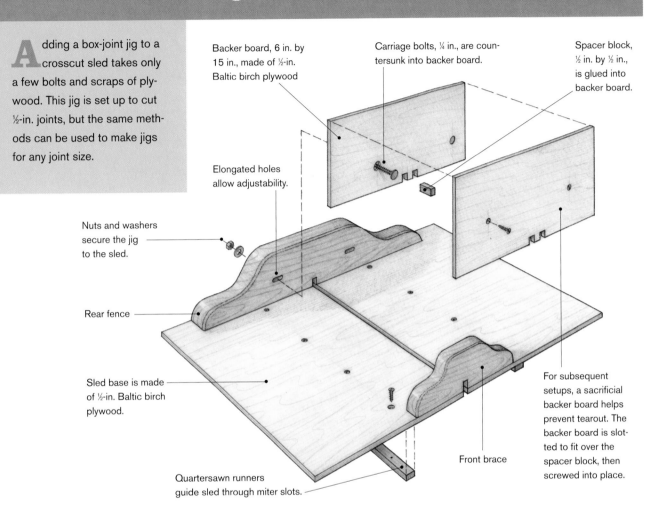

Backer board, 6 in. by 15 in., made of ½-in. Baltic birch plywood

Carriage bolts, ¼ in., are countersunk into backer board.

Spacer block, ½ in. by ½ in., is glued into backer board.

Elongated holes allow adjustability.

Nuts and washers secure the jig to the sled.

Rear fence

Sled base is made of ½-in. Baltic birch plywood.

For subsequent setups, a sacrificial backer board helps prevent tearout. The backer board is slotted to fit over the spacer block, then screwed into place.

Front brace

Quartersawn runners guide sled through miter slots.

starting point—⅛-in.-wide box joints are perfectly fine in ¾-in. material. The thing to remember is that you'll be building a separate jig for each size. And keep in mind that the narrower the box joint, the longer it takes to cut and more likely accumulating error will cause problems.

To make the jig, start by ripping a clear piece of hard maple for a spacer block. Initially, leave it ¹⁄₁₆ in. wider than the size of the joint you're going to make. In this case, the spacer block should be about ⁹⁄₁₆ in. square and long enough to run through a surface planer safely.

One of the critical adjustments is the width of the dado cut. For cutting box joints, you'll need a good stacked dado

set—not the kind that wobbles—that can be reset to the same width easily.

Once the dado is set up, everything else will be adjusted to fit. The width of the dado determines the width of the box joint because both the pin and slot are the same size. As you set up the various blades to cut a ½-in. dado, mark which ones you use and how they are installed so you'll be able to use the same setup next time.

With the dado blades in place, make a new ½-in.-wide slot in the sled. Then you are ready to fit the spacer block. Using the sled, cut a slot in a piece of scrap with the dado, then surface plane the spacer block until it fits tightly in the slot. Next, you'll need a backer board that will bolt to the

SET UP THE DADO BLADE. Use a stacked dado the width of the box joints to cut through the sled. Run a slot through the backer board at the same time.

GLUE THE SPACER BLOCK IN PLACE. Take light cuts on a surface planer until the spacer block fits into the slot in the backer board. Then glue a 2-in. length into place and set aside the assembly to dry.

ADJUST THE JIG. To find a starting point, use the leftover length of spacer material to locate the spacer block ½ in. to the right of the dado blade, then tighten down the bolts.

rear fence. Set the height of the dado above the sled base to match the thickness of the spacer block. Cut two pieces of ½-in. Baltic birch plywood or equivalent, about 8 in. by 14 in., and then cut ½-in.-deep slots with the dado in the center of both pieces on the longest side. Glue a 2-in. piece of the spacer block into the slot on one of the pieces, and set it aside to dry. Make sure the spacer block is square to the backer board, and remove any excess glue while it's still soft. Use ¼-in. carriage bolts to hold the backer board to the sled. Begin by recessing the heads into the birch plywood so they do not protrude. Then drill ¼-in. holes the rest of the way through the plywood.

Set the backer board onto the sled so that the spacer block is about ½ in. to the right of the dado blade, and clamp it in place. Mark the locations for the mounting holes in the sled fence by inserting a pencil through the holes in the backer board. Unclamp the backer board, and lay out holes ¼ in. to the left and to the right of the marks. Drill two ⁵⁄₁₆-in. holes for each bolt, and chisel away the wood between the

holes. Place flat washers under the nuts, then tighten the nuts just enough to draw the carriage bolts into the backer board.

The beauty of this jig is its adjustability. As a starting point, use a piece of the leftover spacer block to locate the pin exactly ½ in. to the right of the dado blade, then tighten down the nuts. A few test joints will lead you to the necessary adjustments.

Cutting Box Joints with the Jig

There are different methods for positioning the pieces with this jig. With the one I suggest, the finished box starts with a full-size joint on its top edge and leaves any partial joints on the bottom.

Begin by setting the height of the dado blade to about ¹⁄₁₆ in. higher than the thickness of the material you're cutting. By setting the height slightly above the thickness, the slots will be deep enough to ensure that the pins will be slightly proud rather than slightly below the surface, allowing you to power sand the joints flush after the glue dries.

Cut a Joint, and Check the Fit

1 Make the first cut. Hold the end piece against the spacer block and backer board, with the top edge facing the spacer block. Cut slowly, and remove the piece before returning the sled to the starting position.

2 Continue cutting the joint. For subsequent cuts, fit the slot over the spacer block, and proceed to the end of the piece.

3 Make the first cut on the side piece. Hold the end piece so that its top edge is against the top edge of the side piece. With the end piece fitted over the spacer block and with its top edge facing the dado blade, position the top edge of the side piece toward the spacer block, and continue cutting.

4 Check the fit; adjust the jig. The corner will be too loose, too tight, or possibly just right. If it's too loose, move the jig slightly to the left. If it's too tight, move it to the right. Tighten the bolts again, then cut another trial corner joint to make sure it's just right.

To prevent tearout on the cuts, the extra slotted backer board you cut earlier will serve as a sacrificial backer board. Position the slot over the spacer block, then screw the sacrificial backer to the jig's backer board. Once all of that is done, it's time to try it out.

Cutting the first joint Cut a strip of Baltic birch plywood about 6 in. wide, then crosscut two pieces about 12 in. long and two more about 8 in. long. This will make a box that you'll use to test and adjust the jig.

Mark the top and bottom edges of each of the pieces so you can orient them correctly as you cut. Mark the long pieces as "sides" and the short ones as "ends."

It's important to note that the piece you're cutting always has its top edge facing to the right. Make the first cut with the top of the first end piece facing the right. Hold the piece against the base of the sled and against the backer board, firmly against the spacer block.

Cut all the way through with the dado blade until the sled hits its stop. Pull the workpiece out of the jig, then return the jig to the starting position. Reposition the end with the slot fitted over the spacer block, and make the next cut. Cut slowly to minimize tearout. Continue until all of the slots are cut on the side piece.

Cuts on the adjacent piece The next step is to cut the joints on one of the side pieces. Use the end piece with its box joints already cut to position the side piece on the jig. Place the first slot cut—the one near the top edge of the end piece—over the spacer block so that the top edge faces to the left. Then place the side piece against the edge of the end piece so that they are aligned top edge to top edge.

With these two pieces in place, make the first cut on the side piece. If the pieces are too small or cumbersome, use clamps to hold them in place. Remove the end piece, and set it aside. Make the rest of the cuts on the side piece the way you did the others on the

end piece, always firmly placing the piece against the spacer block and firmly down on the sled base and against the backer board.

The two pieces should fit together quite easily—neither too tightly nor too loosely—allowing enough room for glue. If your pieces fit together perfectly, congratulations. But chances are the joint will not fit perfectly at this point. Mark the position of the jig before making any adjustment so you know how far to move it. If the joint is too loose, back off the nuts and move the backer board and spacer to the left just a little. If the joints are too tight, move the spacer just slightly to the right.

To make sure the jig is set correctly, it's always a good idea to run a test corner before you cut the joints on your project. Experiment on scrap until the joints fit as they should. Continue to cut individual test corners until the fit is just right. As you work with the jig, its operation will become more familiar.

Putting the Sled Back to Normal Use

A sled's narrow saw-kerf slot ensures accuracy and safety. The edges of a newly cut slot can be used for measuring and setting up, and since it's small, nothing gets caught during a cut. Now it seems like we've ruined the sled by cutting a ½-in.-wide slot down the middle of it. Fortunately, it's a simple matter to close the gap.

Cut a piece of ¼-in. Baltic birch plywood to the size of the sled, and screw it into place using short countersunk screws. With your normal blade back in the tablesaw, cut through the renewed sled base. Mark the plywood inserts with a triangle so you can put them back the same way each time. Now the sled is just like new.

LON SCHLEINING is a woodworker in Dana Point, Calif. He is the author of *Treasure Chests* (2001) and *The Workbench* (2004), both published by The Taunton Press, Inc.

The 60-Minute Toolbox

I'm replacing all of my old metal toolboxes with wooden ones. With the box-joint jig, I can make a box in an hour. I start by gluing up an enclosed box, then cut the lid free on the tablesaw. I add an extra inch to the box height so that I can cut away the lid while still maintaining the full width of the pins. After I'm done, I simply add a piano hinge, handle, and latches. Using this same technique, I've made boxes ranging in size from a few square inches to more than 5 ft. long.

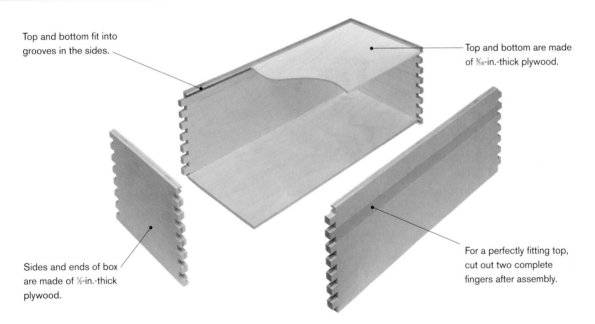

Top and bottom fit into grooves in the sides.

Top and bottom are made of ³⁄₁₆-in.-thick plywood.

Sides and ends of box are made of ½-in.-thick plywood.

For a perfectly fitting top, cut out two complete fingers after assembly.

GLUE UP THE BOX. To speed glue-up, lay out the box parts on a flat surface. Before leaving the assembly, check to see that the box is square, not twisted.

FILL THE VOID. The groove for the top and bottom can be filled easily with end-grain plugs of plywood. Once glued in place, you'll have a hard time spotting the fix.

CUT THE LID FREE. Adding an extra inch to the box height allows you to keep uniform ½-in. pin sizes. Set the blade height just below the thickness of the sides so that the box stays intact during the cutting. Then use a handsaw to separate the top from the bottom.

Tablesawn Dovetails

BY STEVE LATTA

Dovetailing—time-tested, reliable, and strong—is also ornamental and should reflect the personality of the builder. For this to happen, the cabinetmaker must control the number of pins and tails and their size and spacing. Unfortunately, most router dovetailing jigs don't allow for that type of expression. The appearance of the final joint, with thick pins and uniform spacing, is void of personality.

Hand-cutting represents the other end of the spectrum. The size and spacing of the pins are determined by the cabinetmaker. Combine that with the natural irregularities of handwork, and this technique yields a look that is truly wonderful, tying the builder to traditions that are hundreds of years old. However, it requires a great deal of time and skill.

I teach students a tablesaw method that bridges the gap between router-cut and totally hand-cut dovetails. The technique guarantees accuracy while allowing you to control spacing and size. The tails can be as close together as the width of your saw-blade. And it's easy to make the spacing irregular, another sign of handwork.

The main problem my students have with hand-cutting dovetails is crooked saw-cuts, which come back to haunt them when they use the tails to lay out the pins.

Any irregularities create gaps and splits when the boards are joined. Cutting the tails on a tablesaw, using a miter-gauge setup or a guide block riding the rip fence, ensures square cuts. This leads to an accurate transfer and, inevitably, a better joint. The guide-block setup also lets you run a stack of parts in one pass.

Another big advantage is that you spend less time on layout. For multiple dovetails that are identical, the tails need to be marked on only a single piece of stock. The tablesaw setup guarantees repeatability. This also means that pieces are interchangeable, so when running components such as drawer sides, I send a few extra parts along for the ride. If one gets damaged later, a replacement is at hand.

The pins are pretty easy, as long as the layout is transferred accurately with a mark-

Custom-Ground Blade Is the Key

ANGLED TEETH MAKE FOR PERFECT TAIL CUTS. **With the sawteeth ground to the dovetail angle, the blade can be tilted to the same angle, making the top of the cut flush with the scribe line. Only a small triangle of waste stock is left.**

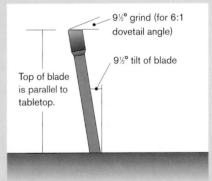

9½° grind (for 6:1 dovetail angle)

9½° tilt of blade

Top of blade is parallel to tabletop.

TABLESAW SETUP INVOLVES A TALL SUPPORT BOARD ATTACHED BETWEEN TWO MITER GAUGES. **A simple stop and clamp allow for accurate repeat cuts.**

ing knife. I use machines to remove the waste between the pins and then pare them by hand, working to the incised line.

Have a Blade Specially Sharpened

Years back I read an article about a cabinet-maker who ground all of the teeth of a tablesaw blade 11½° in one direction and used the blade strictly for dovetailing. Fascinated by this idea, I spent $12★ to have an old narrow-kerf blade ground this way to work with my Unisaw. I had another blade sharpened in the reverse direction to fit my left-tilting Powermatic 66.

When tilted to the proper angle, the top edges of the teeth should be parallel to the surface of the table. Although this tablesaw technique will work with a standard blade, the cut will not reach all the way into the corner. The specially ground blade cuts a perfect corner, leaving only the small triangle of waste between the cuts.

You can have your blade ground to your favorite dovetail angle. I chose a 5:1 angle, which works out to 11½°, but you might prefer 6:1 (9½°) or an 8:1 ratio (7°). The cost of having a blade custom ground is usually under $20 (see "Sources" on p. 77). The blade will handle its light task

Mark and Cut Tails

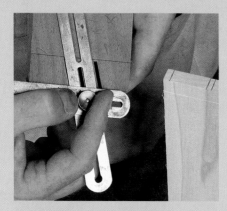

MAKE A TEST CUT TO SET YOUR SLIDING BEVEL TOOL. Use that setting to lay out your dovetails.

THE RIP-FENCE-AND-SUPPORT-BLOCK METHOD WORKS WELL FOR SMALLER PARTS. In this case, the rip fence acts as the stop, making it possible to run up to six parts at a time and keep them aligned.

Four Cuts Are Possible with Each Setup

If the dovetail layout is symmetrical, these setups allow you to make up to four cuts without moving the stop or rip fence. And the dovetails have to be laid out on only one end of one board.

Setup One
Set the rip fence (or stop on the miter-gauge set-up) for the first cut. Rotate and flip the stock for the three corresponding cuts.

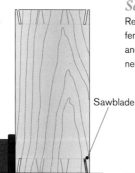

Sawblade

Setup Two
Reset the rip fence (or stop) and make the next four cuts.

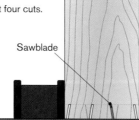

Sawblade

Setup Three
Reset the rip fence for the last four cuts.

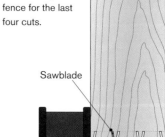

Sawblade

for many years without resharpening. I'm still on my first one.

I recommend using a carbide-tipped blade that has a flat-top grind. Square-tipped teeth like this are common on older blades and blades designed for ripping. The problem with alternate-top-bevel (ATB) teeth is that too much of the carbide may have to be removed to get each tooth down to a common angle, and then the blade may not cut properly. Try telling your local sharpening service what you want; they may be able to work with almost any blade.

Cut the Tails First

When teaching students to cut dovetails, I lay down a simple rule: pencil marks for the tails, knife marks for the pins. Because the tails are cut first, it's no big deal if your cut misses the pencil mark by a little. If it's a scribe line, however, you'll have to cut or pare all the way to that line to remove it and get rid of the small blowouts from severed fibers. Of course, I use a marking gauge to scribe the depths on both the pins and tails boards.

Size matters Basically, I cut the tails by setting the board on end and pushing it through the angled blade. However, depending on the size of the workpiece, I do this in two different ways. For large case pieces, I use drywall screws to attach a support board of medium-density fiberboard (MDF) to a pair of miter gauges, which makes a very stable jig. Then I clamp a stop onto this board to allow repeat cuts. With a very high support board and a waxed table, I've made dovetail cuts on boards standing over 6 ft. tall.

Rather than using a miter-gauge setup for narrow pieces such as drawer sides or drawer stretchers, pieces can be guided by a heavier chunk of stock riding against the rip fence (I save the cutoffs from bedposts for this purpose). This method has a couple

of advantages: It's quicker to set up, and the stop, which is the rip fence in this case, is easier to adjust.

Typically, I'll run each set of drawer sides as a pair, cutting through both simultaneously. For larger-scale jobs, with several drawers equal in height, I often run a stack of six parts in one shot. The rip fence keeps them aligned. Once again, this support block also works to prevent chipout, so make sure each cut goes into fresh stock.

Setting the blade height For through-dovetails, when using the marking gauge to scribe the baseline, go a hair deeper than the thickness of the mating piece. This will cause you to leave the tails slightly proud when the joint comes together; then they can be planed flush to create a perfect appearance. The same should be done for the pins. Half-blind dovetails, however, should be laid out for a flush fit.

Scribe a piece of scrap stock, and use it to fine-tune the blade height. Tilt the blade to the appropriate angle, and raise it slowly, making several test cuts until the blade is cutting right at the line. If you accidentally go too high, reposition the support board or flip the support block. That board or block backs up the cut to prevent chipout.

When the blade is hitting the scribe line exactly, you can use the saw kerf in the scrap piece to set the angle of your adjustable bevel. Lay out the dovetails on your first workpiece. Move the stop block so that the blade lines up with the pencil line, then guide the piece through the cut.

Rabbet the Tails Before Cleaning out the Waste

Before I clean out the waste between the tail cuts, I rabbet the inside edge of the joint. The rabbet is flush with the bottom of the tail sockets and serves a number of purposes. Most important, it makes it much easier to locate the tails board on the pins

Rabbet, Then Remove Waste

RABBET THE TAILS. A small rabbet behind the tails creates a clean inside edge on the finished joint and makes it easier to locate the tails over the pins board when transferring the layout. It also protects the corners of the tails when the boards are stacked.

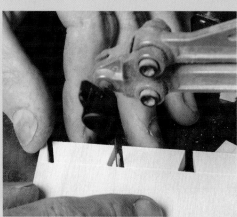

LATTA PREFERS THE SCROLL SAW FOR REMOVING WASTE STOCK BETWEEN TAIL CUTS. He cuts directly across the scribe line, leaving no waste, and the job is done in one step. This waste also can be removed quickly with a chisel.

board, resulting in a precise layout transfer. Rabbeting the tails also leaves a clean corner on the inside of the finished joint, with the shoulder covering blowout, milling errors, and glue squeeze-out.

Cut this rabbet after making the tail cuts. If the rabbet is there first, you will get blowout when cutting the tails. When you put the rabbeted side against the miter fence, there will be no support there for the cut. However, rabbet the tails before cleaning out the waste between the angled table-saw cuts. There will be less waste to clean out, and the rabbet will help guide your chisel if you're chopping by hand.

For small to medium workpieces, make a shoulder that's less than ⅛ in. deep. You can make this cut in a single pass over the tablesaw blade. For carcase pieces or drawer stretchers ⅝ in. or thicker, when the rabbet is thicker than a sawblade, make a shoulder cut followed by a cheek cut on the tablesaw.

It is critical that this rabbet hit the scribe line exactly. Otherwise, the joint won't fit or there will be an unsightly gap on the inside corner. After rabbeting the inside of the tails, don't forget to reset your marking gauge for the pins, which now have less stock to pass through.

Clean out the tails I prefer to use a scrollsaw to cut away the waste. The thin blade can slide sideways down to the base of the tablesaw cut and then cut straight across the bottom in one shot. Cut to the scribe line. It's a waste of time to stay shy of the line and leave the rest for hand-paring.

If you don't have a scrollsaw, waste some of the stock out with a bandsaw and finish with a sharp chisel. Of course, chop only halfway into the workpiece before flipping it over and working in from the other side. Regardless of the method, this step goes quickly—especially if the spacing between the tails (the size of the pins) is kept to a minimum.

Now cut the pins Use a marking knife or X-Acto when transferring the location of the tails to the pins board; a pencil line is just not accurate enough. Also, during the final paring, the tip of your chisel will fall right into the knife mark, leading to a perfect fit.

How you waste out the stock between pins depends on the type of dovetail being cut, the size of the workpieces, and which machines you own.

Three Options for Through-Dovetails

For smaller workpieces, I use a scrollsaw to clean out the waste between the pins. Cut in along the widest part of the pin and across the depth line. With a little practice you will be able to cut right to the scribe line. Having removed the bulk of the waste, use a chisel and marking knife to pare away the remaining triangles of stock.

For larger case pieces with through-dovetails, or when you have a lot of parts to do, use either a router setup or a dado head on the tablesaw. By working with the board set on end, you can use the height adjustment on these machines to establish a clean and square surface at the bottom of these wide spaces.

A router with a straight bit leaves the cleanest cut at the bottom of the pin spaces, and it lets you work closer to the angled cheeks of the pins, but it involves one quick extra step. First clean out most of the material with a scrollsaw or bandsaw. The router will work more smoothly with less material to hog through. Because the router will be riding on the end of the board, clamp on a wide support block. This piece will also back up the cut. Remove as much stock as possible, then pare to your scribed layout lines with a sharp chisel or knife.

On the tablesaw, use the double-miter-gauge setup. I usually stack the dado head to a ½-in. thickness, which doesn't hog away too much material in one pass but still makes the job go quickly. Just as before, if you go too high with your test cuts on scrap, reset the support board so that the cut plows through fresh stock. Place the workpiece so that the widest part of the pin is facing the dado head, that way any blowout will be mostly in a waste area. Again, finish the joint by hand.

Router setup for half-blinds The router-and-support-block setup works well for just about all half-blind dovetails, whether fitting dovetailed stretchers into the tops of table legs, drawer sides into drawer fronts, or case tops and bottoms into sides. Once again, set the router's cutting depth exactly to the scribe line. Finish the pins with a chisel and knife.

Through-Dovetail Pins

TRANSFER THE LAYOUT. The rabbet makes it much easier to keep the boards correctly aligned. Use a knife to mark pins; the scored line will guide your chisel later.

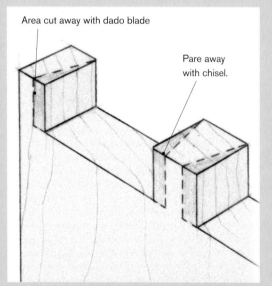

Area cut away with dado blade

Pare away with chisel.

USE A DADO BLADE TO REMOVE AS MUCH STOCK AS POSSIBLE. Again, the rip-fence-and-support-block setup allows multiple workpieces to be run at once.

PARING TO THE LINE. The dado blade (or a router) will leave a square, clean bottom between the pins but small triangles of wood to be pared away. The combination of a chisel and knife works well for paring right to the scribe line and then severing the fibers at the inside corner of the pin.

Half-Blind Dovetails

ROUGH THEM OUT FREEHAND WITH A ROUTER. The end-grain orientation makes it easy to control the cut as you work close to the lines. Clamp the workpiece to an extra block to support the base of the router.

Area cut away with router   Pare away with chisel.

FINISH WITH A SHARP CHISEL. For accurate results when making the final paring cuts, start the chisel in the scored layout marks.

EXPECT A FLAW-LESS FIT. A few light taps should be enough to close the joint.

Method Is a Good Compromise

I'd love to teach my students to cut all of their dovetails by hand, cherishing both the process and final product. But their skill levels and the reality of the marketplace they're entering simply won't allow for that. The structural integrity and final appearance of the joint is what matters most. With this tablesaw technique, you get most of the character of a hand-cut joint in much less time. All in all, it's a compromise I can live with.

*Please note price estimates are from 2001.

STEVE LATTA is a furniture-making instructor at the Thaddeus Stevens College of Technology in Lancaster, Penn.

Sources

Forrest Manufacturing
Phone: (800) 733-7111
www.Forrest.wood
mall.com

Freud Manufacturing
Phone: (800) 472-7307
www.freudtools.com

Machine Dovetails by Eye

BY JEFF MILLER

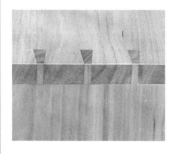

I like cutting dovetails by hand, but the nature of my business doesn't let me stay in practice. And I admit, I tend to lose a little accuracy when I'm out of shape. I've tried router jigs, but I've never found one I like. I find them fussy to set up, and to my eye, router-cut dovetails never look as good as those cut by hand.

Some years ago, a friend showed me a way to use my tablesaw and bandsaw to make dovetails that look hand cut. The jig is surprisingly fast to set up, and it lets me cut

dovetails of any size and spacing. It's not a production jig, but it's fast enough to use in a professional shop, and it works well in limited production situations. Disadvantages? The quality of the fit will depend on your ability to cut accurately to a line. But I like that; I find it far more satisfying than using a dovetail jig. In some ways, this is still a hand-cut procedure. (I can hear the traditionalists howl.) The finished joint certainly looks as if it's been hand cut (see the photo on p. 82).

Tablesaw Jig for Cutting Dovetails

This simple sled is the key to efficient machine dovetails that look hand cut. Pins are cut in two passes on the jig, one on each side. The author cuts the tails on the bandsaw.

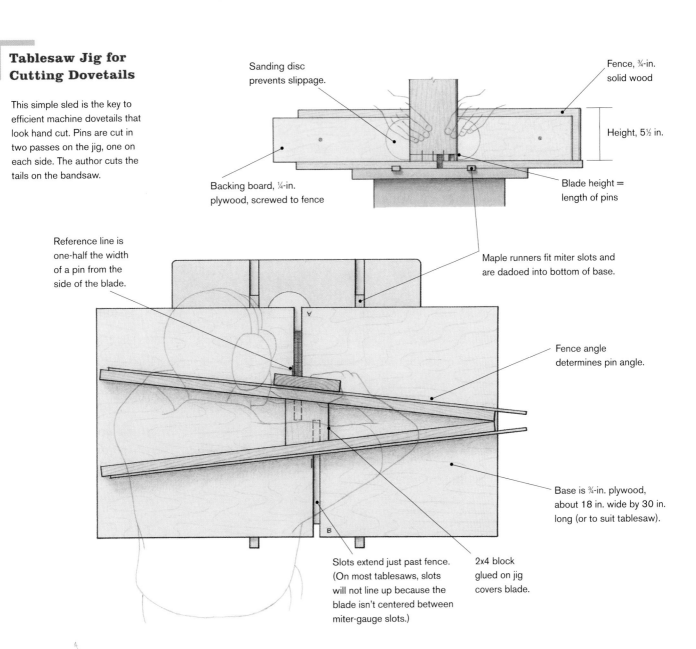

Sanding disc prevents slippage.

Fence, ¾-in. solid wood

Height, 5½ in.

Backing board, ¼-in. plywood, screwed to fence

Blade height = length of pins

Reference line is one-half the width of a pin from the side of the blade.

Maple runners fit miter slots and are dadoed into bottom of base.

Fence angle determines pin angle.

Base is ¾-in. plywood, about 18 in. wide by 30 in. long (or to suit tablesaw).

Slots extend just past fence. (On most tablesaws, slots will not line up because the blade isn't centered between miter-gauge slots.)

2x4 block glued on jig covers blade.

A Simple Jig Cuts the Pins

The key to this method is a tablesaw jig for cutting the pins. Two fences angled to a narrow V-shape are mounted on a sled that runs in the miter-gauge slots of my tablesaw. I make the pins in two passes over a ½-in. dado cutter (see the photo on the facing page). With the first pass, I cut one side of each pin. Then I rotate the sled, and cut the other side. I use the pins to mark the tails before cutting them on the bandsaw.

The base of the sled is made of ¾-in. plywood, 18 in. wide by 30 in. long (see the drawing above). The runners for the miter slots are glued into shallow dadoes on the bottom of the sled. To ensure the dadoes are parallel to one another, I run the same edge against the fence while cutting each dado.

The fences are set at 6° off a line drawn perpendicular to the blade, which gives a pin angle of 6°. This is a 9:1 ratio. I picked that angle simply because I think it looks

Cutting Pins with the Jig

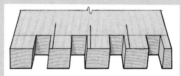

MAKE THE PINS IN TWO PASSES OVER A DADO CUTTER. The first pass cuts one side of each pin. The author aligns the centers of the pins with the pencil mark on one side of the sled.

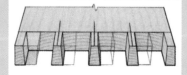

THE SECOND SET OF CUTS FINISHES THE PINS. After cutting one side of each pin, rotate the jig 180°, and cut the angle on the other side. Align the centers of the pins with the reference mark on the other side of the sled.

best. I recently discovered the jig I had been using for years had one fence set at 6°, the other at 8°. I never noticed until I measured it for drawings. The lesson: Don't worry too much about the angle.

The fences are made of ¾-in. solid wood, 5¾ in. high and fastened from below with screws. Because the blade cuts through the sled between the fences, I glued a block into the space as a guard. After cutting a few dadoes of different widths and heights, the fence was chewed up in the area of the blade. So I mounted ¼-in. plywood backing boards on the fences to prevent tearout. I move the backing boards each time I change the dovetail profile and replace them when necessary. Sanding discs glued to the backing boards keep the pin board from slipping. Just make sure that the discs are not in the path of the cut or sparks will fly.

Jig Setup Is Based on Pin Width

Laying out the dovetails is simple. As I do with hand-cut dovetails, I use a marking knife to scribe a line on both faces of the board to locate the bottoms of the pins and to help prevent tearout on the waste portion. I set the dado cutter so the depth of cut just touches the scribed line. On the outside face of the board, I mark the centerlines of the pins. I space them evenly, but you can space them any way you like. The angle of the cut is set by the angle of the fences; the width of the pins is up to you.

I made a pencil line on each side of the jig to determine pin width. The distance from the pencil lines to the cutter is half the width of the pins. When cutting, I align each layout line on the pin board with the pencil line on the jig.

The first round of tablesaw cuts puts the angle on one side of the pins. I line up the reference marks, as shown in the top photo at left, run the sled through the blade and repeat at the next mark. I like the half pins at each end to be close to full width, so I

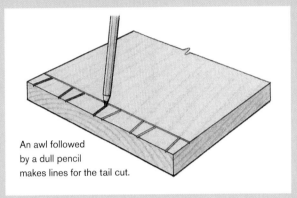

An awl followed by a dull pencil makes lines for the tail cut.

USE AN AWL TO MARK THE TAILS FROM THE PINS. The author supports the pieces on his jointer as he scribes the marks for the tail cuts.

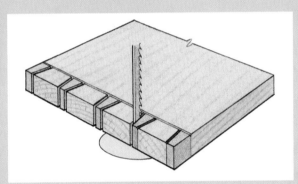

A BANDSAW COMPLETES THE JOB. Cut to the lines on each side of the tails, and then nibble away the waste. Take care not to cut beyond the scribed baseline.

align the edge of the board with an imaginary line that's twice as far from the blade as the reference mark. When I've cut one side of all the pins, I turn off the saw and rotate the jig 180° to cut the other side of the pins at the opposing angle (see the bottom photo on the facing page). If there's any waste left between the two cuts, I scoot the board over and make another pass.

A Bandsaw Cuts the Tails

The first step in laying out the tails is to scribe a baseline across both sides of the end of the board with a marking knife. Then the tails are scribed with a sharp awl. I do the marking on my jointer because it has a handy right-angle surface (see the top photo above). The outside face of the tail board goes down on the jointer table, and the pin board stands on it with the marked

face (outside) against the fence. Before I go any further, I label all the mating pieces to avoid confusion.

Cutting the tails is nothing more than cutting to the line on the bandsaw. And this is the crucial task here. In the woodworking classes I teach, many beginners have trouble cutting to a line. There are three things that go into cutting to a line accurately: sharpening the perception of the line, sharpening the perception of the cut, and practicing to get the two to meet.

Consider the line first. I like a scribed line because it makes a precise mark, as long as the scribe is made with consistent pressure. A scribed line is actually a little canyon cut into the wood. To make this clearer, I have students trace the scribed lines with a dull pencil (see the top drawing on p. 81). The result is two pencil lines, one on either side of the impression left by the scribe. Cut away one of the pencil lines, and you've cut to the line.

I cut sides of the tails to the line and use the blade to nibble away the rest of the waste, being careful to stop at the scribed baseline (see the bottom photo on p. 81). I rotate the piece 90° and cut along the scribed line for the bottoms of the half-pins at the ends. Slightly ragged bottoms on the tail can be cleaned up with a chisel. After some practice, you can dispense with this step.

The Moment of Truth

The first few times I cut dovetails this way, the fit was a little tight, and I had to pare the high spots with a chisel. If one section is loose, a small wedge glued in place can make an almost invisible repair. Sanding dust mixed with finish can make a good joint look almost perfect.

JEFF MILLER's Chicago studio serves as shop, showroom, and classroom for his woodworking courses.

Shopmade Tenoning Jig

BY BRAD SCHILLING

The mortise and tenon is one of the most common woodworking joints. So a good tablesaw tenoning jig is a valuable tool for the shop. But top-quality, commercially made jigs don't come cheap. When I was faced with cutting a bunch of tenons, I decided to build a jig that included all of the features found in a top-of-the-line model.

The jig has a tall fence to support the workpiece. And a heavy-duty hold-down keeps the stock securely in place. To minimize tearout, a narrow piece of scrap stock can be temporarily clamped in front of the workpiece. The jig slides smoothly along the table of the saw without side-to-side play. And a threaded rod with a crank allows easy and accurate adjustment of the work-piece relative to the blade.

Once I worked out the design and bought the parts (see "Sources" on p. 86), I put together the jig in only a few hours. My total cash outlay for everything was about $40, inexpensive compared with a store-bought jig with the same features.

The jig is made of ¾-in.-thick medium-density fiberboard (MDF), a smooth material that tends to stay flat and is reasonably inexpensive. Keep in mind that the jig is sized for my Delta Unisaw. However, it can fit almost any saw simply by adjusting the length of the base as needed.

One more point before starting. Most of the parts of this jig are cut on the tablesaw. That means the saw must be cutting accurately. If it isn't, the jig won't have the built-in precision that's needed to make perfect cuts. So, before you get going, make sure the blade and rip fence are parallel to the miter-gauge slot and that the blade is square to the table.

Rip the Runners First

When the jig is in use, it's guided by an ultrahigh molecular weight (UHMW) plastic runner (see "Sources" on p. 86) that travels along the saw's miter-gauge slot and fits in a groove in the jig's base. Cut the runner for a snug sliding fit in the slot. If the runner doesn't fit snugly, it can shift as it slides. While you're at it, cut the two plastic runners that mount to the platform. By the way, any good combination blade will produce a smooth cut in UHMW plastic.

RIP THE PLASTIC RUNNERS. A combination blade makes a smooth cut in UHMW plastic.

CUT SOME GROOVES. A dado head plows a pair of parallel grooves in an oversize blank.

Cut the MDF Parts

With the runners cut, you can start working on the MDF base and platform. Because these two parts have a pair of parallel grooves that need to align when the jig is assembled, cut both parts from an oversize blank—a single piece of MDF, 14 in. wide by 24 in. long. That way the grooves in both parts can be cut at the same time to ensure alignment.

This is also a good time to cut the remaining grooves. The groove on the underside of the base accepts the miter-gauge runner. The groove on the back face of the fence accepts the platform.

Now cut the blank into two parts: one 9¼ in. long for the platform and one 13 in. long for the base. The connecting block and the support block work together as part of the micro-adjust system. Both of these parts have a hole bored on one face, with each hole drilled just deep enough to accept a washer and nut. When the two parts have been assembled, the holes create a pocket that accepts both washers and nuts.

I used a router with an edge guide to cut the slot in the platform for the carriage bolt. Before routing, I drilled a ⁵⁄₁₆-in.-diameter hole to provide a starting point for a ¼-in.-diameter straight bit. The head of the carriage bolt is recessed in a counter-bore in the underside of the base. Now add the threaded insert to the crank block. Drill a ½-in.-diameter hole, lubricate the outside threads of the insert with wax, and screw it in place.

CUT THE BLANK IN TWO. **Crosscutting the blank provides stock for the base and platform.**

Tablesaw Tenoning Jig

With a heavy-duty hold-down; an extra-tall fence; and a large, stable base, the tenoning jig provides a good measure of control and safety during a cut. MDF parts (all ¾ in. thick) are smooth and stay flat. Runners made from UHMW plastic slide smoothly.

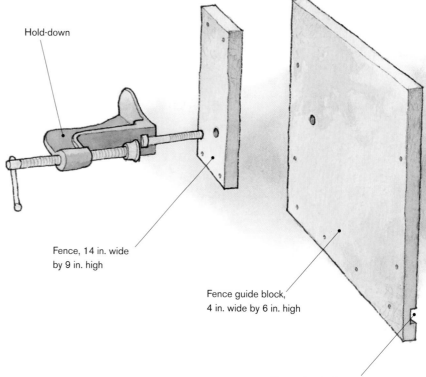

Hold-down

Fence, 14 in. wide by 9 in. high

Fence guide block, 4 in. wide by 6 in. high

Groove for platform, ⅜ in. deep by ¾ in. wide

Assemble and Finish

At this point, all of the MDF parts can be screwed together. Keep in mind, though, that MDF tends to split, especially when screwing into an edge. So it's important to drill pilot holes before adding screws.

After that, cut the three runners to final length. Then drill, countersink, and screw each runner in place.

The micro–adjust system comes next. Cut the threaded rod to length. Then add the crank, nuts, and washers. To complete the system, it's just a matter of screwing the connecting block to the support block.

To add moisture protection to the jig, it's a good idea to apply a couple of coats of polyurethane to the MDF parts. Mounting the hold–down completes the jig.

★Please note price estimates are from 2002.

BRAD SCHILLING enjoys working wood in Fairview Heights, Ill.

Sources

Reid Tool
2265 Black Creek Rd.
Muskegon, MI 49444
Phone: (800) 253-0421
Web: www.reidtool.com
Crank (part No. JCL-1160)
Knob (part No. DK-167)

Rockler Woodworking and Hardware
4365 Willow Dr.
Medina, MN 55340
Phone: (800) 279-4441
Web: www.rockler.com
3-in. hold-down and UHMW plastic

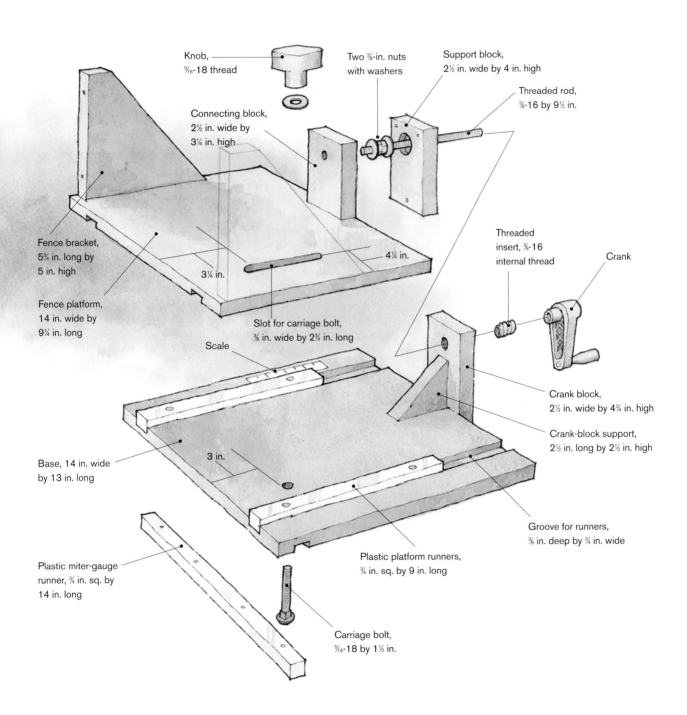

Knob,
⁵⁄₁₆-18 thread

Two ⅜-in. nuts
with washers

Support block,
2½ in. wide by 4 in. high

Threaded rod,
⅜-16 by 9½ in.

Connecting block,
2½ in. wide by
3¼ in. high

Fence bracket,
5¾ in. long by
5 in. high

4¼ in.

Threaded
insert, ⅜-16
internal thread

Crank

3¼ in.

Fence platform,
14 in. wide by
9¼ in. long

Slot for carriage bolt,
⅜ in. wide by 2¾ in. long

Scale

Crank block,
2½ in. wide by 4¾ in. high

Crank-block support,
2½ in. long by 2½ in. high

Base, 14 in. wide
by 13 in. long

3 in.

Groove for runners,
⅜ in. deep by ¾ in. wide

Plastic platform runners,
¾ in. sq. by 9 in. long

Plastic miter-gauge
runner, ¾ in. sq. by
14 in. long

Carriage bolt,
⁵⁄₁₆-18 by 1½ in.

Angled Tenons on the Tablesaw

BY WILLIAM KRASE

ANGLED TENONS can be difficult to cut, especially if they're compound. Krase's system greatly simplifies the process. The workpiece seats securely against the wedges at the juncture of the crossfeed and sliding table, while the sliding table guides the whole affair through the blade.

L ots of furniture—especially pieces intended to accommodate the human body—require joints that are not square. Chairs may have as many as 16 such joints, some of which are compound (angled in two planes). That's why chairs can be difficult. They don't have to be.

With my addition of a crossfeed box to Kelly Mehler's sliding table and the use of

purpose-made wedges, you can cut even compound-angled tenons quickly, accurately, time after time (see the photo above). The wedges establish the tenon angle while the crossfeed box positions the workpiece to get the correct length, width, and thickness of tenon.

I arrived at this method of cutting angled tenons because I wanted to make the stool in the photo below. Since then, I've used it on four more pieces of furniture—over 60 angled joints in all. Though now I wish I'd made the sliding table and crossfeed box of a better material, I've been completely satisfied with both the apparatus and the results.

I used regular particleboard (the kind often used for floor underlayment) for the sliding table's base and for the crossfeed box. Particleboard is what I had handy, but if I were to build another, I'd use medium-density fiberboard (MDF) or a good-quality birch plywood instead. Particleboard seems to be susceptible to changes in humidity, resulting in some binding whenever the humidity becomes extreme.

I make wedges for projects as I need them. They must be long enough to support the workpiece securely in the upright position. I've found that 1-ft. sections of 2x stock work well.

To make the thumbscrews that fasten the crossfeed box to the sliding table, I bought a length of ⅟₁₆-in. by ½-in. brass strip (from a hobby shop), cut pieces to size, and soldered them into the head slots of slotted brass machine screws. The resulting home-made thumbscrews are oversize, so it's easy to tighten the crossfeed box in place. I use large washers beneath the thumbscrews to prevent them from digging into the cross-feed box.

Cutting Tenons

Generally, the first thing I do when cutting angled tenons is to cut the end of the workpiece parallel to what will be the shoulder of the tenon, using the sliding table and wedges. Then, when I position the wedge (or wedges), I make sure the end of the workpiece flushes up against the crossfeed box (for cutting shoulders) or the base of the sliding table (for the cheeks). This helps orient the workpiece and minimizes the chance of my ending up with an

expensive piece of kindling. That's happened only once using this jig, when I measured to the wrong side of the sawblade.

Tenons angled in one plane require one wedge; compound-angled tenons require two. I use the same wedges for cutting both the shoulders and the cheeks. The wedges just have to be manipulated to reposition the workpiece properly with respect to the blade—in practice, the orientation is obvious. As a rule, I cut the shoulders first and then the cheeks. This creates a crisp shoulder, makes cutting the cheeks easier, and minimizes the chance of pinching the blade with the small offcuts.

With the workpiece bearing against two surfaces oriented 90° to each other and with the force of the blade serving to seat the workpiece only more securely, I'm comfortable handholding the workpiece. If it makes you feel safer or more secure, by all means, use a clamp, but just be sure the clamp doesn't vibrate loose and fall into the blade.

WILLIAM KRASE is a retired aerospace engineer who builds furniture and boats in Mendocino, Calif.

ANGLED TENONS. This walnut furniture is joined almost exclusively with angled tenons, including some compound tenons. Legs on two of these pieces splay in two directions, requiring slightly angled tenons at both ends of apron pieces, stretchers, and seat supports.

Joinery for Curved Work

BY GARRETT HACK

Many of us began our wood working journey by building Shaker and Craftsman furniture. The predominantly square edges and flat surfaces common to these styles are ideal for laying out and cutting accurate joinery. But as you mature as a woodworker, you may wish to make curves a part of your repertoire, too.

The slightest curve adds elegance to any furniture design. To my eye, straight lines are nowhere as interesting as curved lines, which capture the imagination. Curved parts can add physical strength to a design while preserving its visual lightness.

Curved surfaces open a whole new realm of furniture styles: Chippendale, Federal, and Hepplewhite, for starters. Yes, curves add complexity, especially when it comes to joinery. But with full-scale drawings and custom-made jigs, you can work out the problems of angled joints and cut them using machines and hand tools.

Full-Scale Drawings Are Crucial

It is difficult to visualize the joinery of curved parts without making drawings. I often start with quarter-scale drawings to work out the overall design, then move on

FULL-SCALE DRAWINGS help eliminate mistakes, help one figure out exactly how a piece goes together, and can be used to transfer layout marks onto stock.

Mortising Curved Parts

MACHINE MORTISING.
To cut an angled mortise with a horizontal mortiser, orient the stock using angled wedges. The same method will work if you use a vertically mounted hollow-chisel mortiser.

Mortise Options

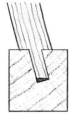

By Machine   *By Hand*

It's easier to cut an angled mortise (left) using a machine. When chopping a mortise by hand, it's easier to keep the mortise straight. Be aware that a severe angle on the tenon may result in weak, short grain.

WHEN POSSIBLE, DESIGN A JOINT TO COME TOGETHER WITH FLAT MATING SURFACES. Using a block plane, the author planes a flat spot where this compound-curve laminated leg mates with a chair rail.

MARK THE MORTISE USING THE MATCHING PIECE. Layout marks are trans- ferred from a chair rail onto the leg.

CUT THE MORTISE. Depending on the shape of the piece, sometimes it's easier to clamp the workpiece in a vise and chop the mortise by hand than it is to build a complex jig to hold it steady for machining.

Tenoning Curved Part

A combination of machines, shopmade jigs, and hand tools are often required to cut tenons on curved parts.

1 Use a full-scale drawing to transfer layout marks to a curved piece. The line to the immediate right of the ruler is an extension of the tenon. The one next to it is a parallel line. Sight the ruler by eye, using the lines for guides, and mark the tenon.

2 Mark the shoulder. Hold a sliding bevel gauge steady against the concave section of a curved piece, such as this table apron.

3 A large, curved part needs a jig to hold it steady when cutting tenons. Cut a large shim that mates to a curved part and use the tablesaw's rip fence as a guide when cutting a tenon. Attach the shim using tape.

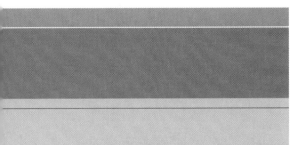

4 Cut an angled shoulder using a hand-saw held at the correct angle. Refer to the layout marks on the top and edges of the stock when guiding the saw (left).

5 Clean up the shoulder using a hand-plane.

to full-scale drawings to figure out the particulars, which includes joinery.

A project may require one or more views. Two-dimensional curves, such as the edge of a tabletop or the rails of a chair, can be fully rendered in a top (plan) view. The curving back leg of a chair, a common three-dimensional shape, usually requires both front and side views to be fully visualized.

For laying out curves, I use thin, flexible wood battens. A typical batten is about ¾ in. wide and ⁄₁₆ in. thick and is made of a good bending wood such as oak or ash. A steel ruler also works, but it's not very flexible for tight curves. Besides, I prefer the natural curve of a wooden batten. Perhaps I get a slightly less precise curve than I would with a steel ruler, but that is, after all, the way the wooden parts themselves behave when steam-bending or laminating.

The dilemma of working with curved parts is that they often end up meeting at odd angles. Try to make all of your joinery decisions during the drawing stage, including whether you wish to angle mortises, tenons, or both. As a rule, I prefer to angle the mortise and keep the tenon at right angles to its shoulders. That rule is based on the fact that it's easy to get an angled mortise using a horizontal mortiser or a hollow-chisel mortiser. But if I were to cut mortises by hand, I'd lean toward keeping the mortises square because it's tough to chop at a consistent angle using chisels.

During the design stage, it's important to visualize how the piece will be assembled. Can you get all of those angled joints together in an orderly progression without stressing some part? And is there a way to jig a part to make the necessary cuts?

Once the drawings are complete, it's a good idea to make patterns of some parts using thin, flexible pieces of wood or plywood. Flexible patterns make it easy to transfer layout marks onto parts, especially when dealing with pieces that have compound curves.

Use Shims while Cutting Mortises

Mortises are cut first because it's a lot easier to handplane a tenon to fit than it is to enlarge a mortise by a whisker. I use an old horizontal mortiser modified to accept a router for cutting mortises.

Although the sliding table doesn't tilt, I have no trouble cutting angled mortises. I make up wedges or use shims to hold the workpiece at the proper angle. If you use a hollow-chisel mortiser, the same techniques would apply.

Transfer layout marks for the mortises directly from the drawing or from patterns you've copied from the drawing. On a part with compound curves, it's best to use a pattern that can be clamped to the part, then transfer layout marks.

Steam-bent or laminated parts with compound curves usually do not have any true flat surfaces, which can make it difficult to mark out joints accurately as well as to cut parts that mate tightly. To overcome this difficulty, once I've steam-bent or laminated the parts, I plane small flats at the joints. Take, for example, the laminated rear leg of a chair (see the photos on the facing page). After the glue dries, clean up the leg using handplanes. Then use a pattern taken from the drawing to mark the location of joints. Don't mark all of the joinery at once. First, mark the outside edges of where the rail meets the leg. Then plane that section flat, which makes it possible to rest a square or bevel gauge solidly to both lay out the joint and check it as you cut. Shoulder lines will then be straight and a lot easier to cut than if they were curved. At a minimum, I like to leave a flat surface and one—or preferably two—edges square to it.

Once the area has been planed flat, finish the layout and cut the joint. When working with oddly shaped parts, it may be easier to hand-chop a few mortises than it would be to make a complicated hold-down jig. It depends on how many duplicate parts are required in a project.

Parts To Be Tenoned also Require Hold-Down Devices

Curved work frequently relies on parts made from laminations or steam bending. These parts are generally formed before you can lay out and cut the joinery.

Once the part has been formed, check to see whether it indeed follows the drawing exactly. If it does not, don't worry. Steam-bent or laminated parts don't always obey drawings. If there's a slight deviation due to springback, make changes using the actual part as a drawing template and revise the angles of joints if necessary.

Although I make patterns of many curved parts to aid in transferring layout marks, often all that's necessary is the drawing itself. Just lay parts on the drawing and transfer the layout (see the photos on pp. 92–93). I often add extra lines to the drawing to help with transferring layout lines. For example, in the case of an angled tenon on a curved apron, I extend the lines marking the tenons as well as add a line parallel to it. That way, I can lay a ruler on top of the apron, line it up with the extra lines of the drawing and accurately mark the locations of the tenons.

I prefer to cut tenons on the tablesaw. I have a tenoning jig that works fine with square stock. If possible, I cut tenons using the jig before shaping the curve. But when working with already curved pieces, I have to get inventive.

A wide, laminated table apron won't fit in a tenoning jig no matter how hard you try. To cut the tenons on a piece like this on a tablesaw, find some scrap and cut a large shim that will allow you to guide the workpiece safely along the saw's rip fence. Attach the shim to the workpiece with masking tape or double-sided tape.

If the workpiece is small and curved slightly, such as a rail of a chair, I make a jig

Using a Tenon Jig

WHEN POSSIBLE, CUT JOINTS BEFORE CUTTING ALL OF THE CURVES. This chair rail still has one flat face, which goes against the tenoning jig. Bandsaw the convex curve after cutting the tenons.

IF PARTS ARE LAMINATED OR STEAM-BENT, MAKE A JIG FOR A JIG. A simple jig supports this curved piece at the correct angle and still makes it possible to use a tenoning jig.

that lets me use my tenoning jig (see the right photo above). Whenever possible, I design the piece and the jig so that the tenon is cut with the tablesaw blade at 90°. Some designs, however, necessitate tilting the blade, too.

Once the cheeks have been cut, go back to the drawing and transfer layout marks for the shoulders. If the shoulders are angled, transfer the angle using a sliding bevel gauge and marking knife. Cut the shoulders a hair proud using a handsaw, and trim them to the line using a shoulder plane.

In the construction of complex, curved work, there are bound to be slight deviations from the drawing. Take time to see how parts are fitting together, and be prepared to make changes. I call this working from reality. Dry-fit parts as you go, and make a new pattern for an adjoining part if something is off slightly. This is good advice in much of furniture building. Using an accurate pattern is a good strategy whenever you have a tricky part to fit.

GARRETT HACK is an author, furniture maker and teacher from Thetford Center, Vt.

Dust-Proof Your Contractor's Saw

BY DICK MCDONOUGH

Whenever I'm doing a lot of ripping and crosscutting with my saw, I generate a blizzard of airborne sawdust. So to prevent all of that sawdust from filling my shop (and lungs), I mounted a small plywood box under the saw cabinet and connected the box to my dust collector. And to prevent dust from blowing out through the wide-open back of the cabinet, I covered most of the open area with a piece of plywood.

Now when I fire up my dust collector, I'm able to collect 95 percent of the dust generated by the tablesaw. My shop is considerably cleaner. And so, too, is my dust mask.

In my case, the dust box is mounted to a Delta 10-in. contractor's saw. But the basic idea here is adaptable to just about any contractor-type saw.

Gaps Must Be Filled First

Before starting on the box, I filled the gaps in the joint between the top of the cabinet and the underside of the table with 1¼-in. by 1¼-in. nonadhesive-backed weather stripping (available at hardware stores).

If you see gaps where the top of the stand meets the underside of the cabinet, fill them with ³⁄₁₆-in. by ½-in. adhesive-backed weather stripping. After loosening the bolts that hold the saw cabinet to the stand, slip the weather stripping under the bottom edge of the cabinet, pressing the adhesive surface all along the joint line. When the cabinet is lowered onto the stripping, you end up with a nice seal.

Ramps Keep Dust off Ledges

At the inside bottom edge of the cabinet, the sides bend in to create a horizontal surface for mounting the cabinet to a stand or base. Also, some commercially made stands

A Simple Box Does the Job

A tapered box funnels tablesaw dust straight into a dust collector. (Dimensions based on a Delta 10-in. contractor's saw.)

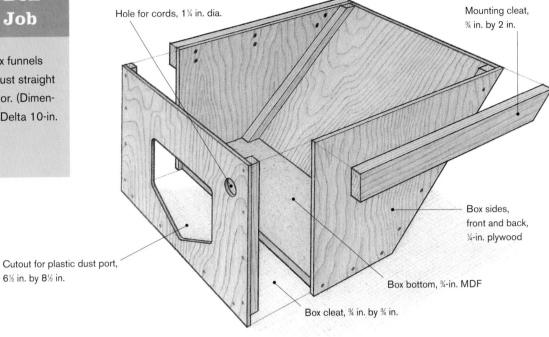

Hole for cords, 1¼ in. dia.

Mounting cleat, ¾ in. by 2 in.

Cutout for plastic dust port, 6½ in. by 8½ in.

Box sides, front and back, ¼-in. plywood

Box bottom, ¾-in. MDF

Box cleat, ¾ in. by ¾ in.

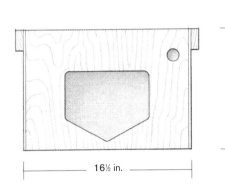

Back View

16½ in.

11½ in.

Side View

19 in.

7½ in.

NO FANCY JOINERY REQUIRED. The author uses ring-shank nails to join the dust-box parts.

THE DUST PORT GOES ON BACK. A plastic dust port provides an easily accessible attachment point for the dust-collector hose.

JACK IT UP. An old scissors jack holds the dust box in place when driving home the sheet-metal screws.

A Back Plate Improves Efficiency

Mounting a plate to the back of the saw cabinet helps contain the dust. (Dimensions based on a Delta 10-in. contractor's saw.)

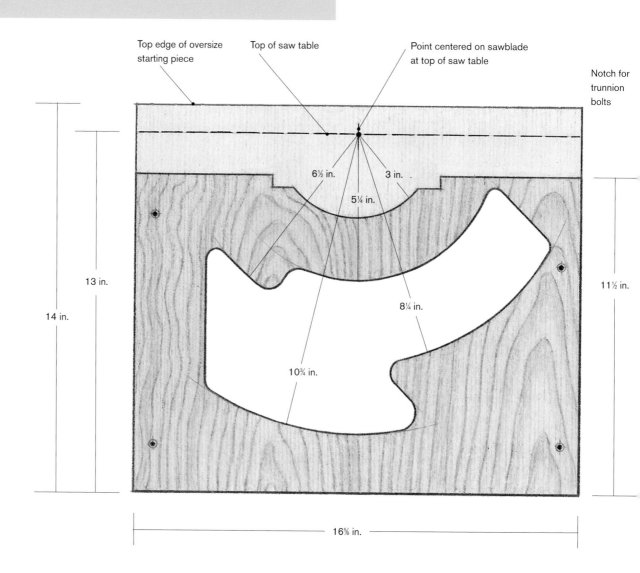

Top edge of oversize starting piece

Top of saw table

Point centered on sawblade at top of saw table

Notch for trunnion bolts

6½ in.

3 in.

5¼ in.

13 in.

14 in.

8¼ in.

11½ in.

10¾ in.

16⅝ in.

have a top surface with an opening in the center to let the dust fall through. In both cases, four ledges are created around the bottom of the cabinet.

Unfortunately, these ledges are a perfect place for unwanted sawdust to accumulate and become a nuisance. To solve the problem, I screwed an angled scrap of wood to each of the four ledges. These "ramps" allow the dust to fall off the ledges easily and down into the dust box.

Dust Box Directs Dust to the Hose

I could have connected my dust-collector hose to a port mounted directly on the bottom of the saw cabinet. But because I often remove the hose and temporarily attach it to other machines, I wanted the port to be easily accessible. So by adding a box under the saw cabinet, I was able to mount a plastic dust port (with a 4-in. outlet) that sticks

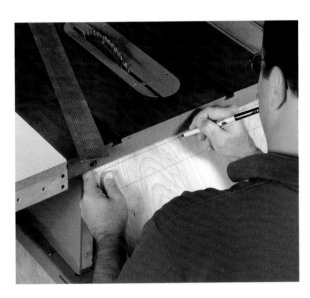

TRANSFER THE MARK. Slip the back plate under the top of the saw to transfer the center point of the arc from the saw to the plate.

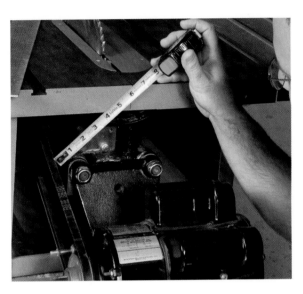

MEASURE THE BELT IN THE RAISED POSITION. Take the first measurement with the sawblade in its highest position.

SCRIBE THE ARCS. Establish the upper and lower edges of the cutout by scribing the arcs with a compass.

CUT OUT THE OPENING. To achieve a nice radius, drill ¾-in.-diameter holes in the corners before cutting out the opening with a sabersaw.

ADD THE BACK PLATE. **With the motor removed to allow for easier access, slip the plate in place and secure it with a few sheet-metal screws.**

straight out the back. That way I can get at the port with little effort. And to attach the hose, I just slip it onto the port and tighten an automotive hose clamp.

The box itself is mostly ¼-in.-thick plywood, with a ¾-in.-thick medium-density fiberboard (MDF) bottom and a few pine cleats. Tapering the sides of the box helps direct the dust into the port.

There's nothing fussy about joining the parts for the dust box. Once the opening in the back piece (for the dust port) has been cut out with a sabersaw, you just nail or screw the parts in place. Start by attaching the four box cleats. Position them flush with the edges of the front and back pieces, and attach them with ring-shank nails. After that, cut the bottom to size, and bevel its front edge to match the taper of the sides. Then nail the ¼-in.-thick plywood sides to the bottom. To complete the box, nail through the sides and into the box cleats in the back and front.

Mounting the dust box to the stand is a pretty simple step. The mounting cleats are screwed flush with the top edge of the

sides. And after drilling a 1¼-in.-diameter access hole for the power cords, the plastic dust port is screwed to the back. The dust port is available from Woodworker's Supply (part number 894-738; see "Sources" on the facing page). Then the mounting cleats are attached to the stand by driving sheet-metal screws through the stand and down into the cleats. On some saws you might have to screw through the sides of the cabinet into the side of each mounting cleat.

Back Plate Helps Keep Dust in the Box

The dust collector works most efficiently when the back of the saw cabinet is at least partially covered. From my experience, if the back is totally uncovered, some of the dust manages to find its way out through the slot for the handwheel or the sawblade slot in the tablesaw insert. So to help cover the open back of the cabinet, I added a back plate made of ¼-in.-thick plywood.

The back plate mounts directly to the back of the saw. But it's not quite as simple as cutting the plywood to size and screwing it in place. Because the drive belt and motor mount extend out the back of the saw, some of the plate must be cut away.

Figuring out what portion to remove could be tricky, because the belt and motor mount must be able to move up and down when you're changing the height of the sawblade. Then, too, the belt and motor mount swing in an arc from 0° to 45°. But if you take a few minutes to do some layout, it's a pretty straightforward procedure.

Looking straight at the back of the saw, you can see the arc of travel that's followed by the belt and motor mount. This arc has a radius with a center point that aligns dead-on with the center of the sawblade and the top of the saw table. So it's a good idea to start by marking this point on the back edge of your saw.

It will be easier to lay out the opening on the back plate if you cut the plate to a height that equals the distance from the top of the stand to the top of the saw table, plus about 1 in. Don't worry about that extra material. For now, you want the top edge of the plate to extend above the table.

At this point, it's okay to cut the back plate to its final width. Simply measure from one side of the saw to the other and cut the plate to the measured dimension. Then draw a couple of straight lines across the plywood to represent the location of the top and bottom surfaces of the tablesaw. Now you can place the top edge of the plate against the top of the saw table and transfer the location of the center point of the arc from the table to the upper line just drawn on the plywood. Make sure the ends of the plywood are flush with the sides of the saw cabinet.

Once the arc center point has been marked on the back plate, you're ready to scribe the cutout for the belt and the motor mount. First, take measurements directly from the back of the saw. Second, transfer these points to the back plate. And third, use these points to set the compass and scribe the various arcs on the plate.

Start by marking the points for the belt. To do that, raise the blade to its highest point, and measure from the center point on the back of the saw table to the top of the belt. Subtract ³⁄₁₆ in. or so for clearance, and mark this point on the back plate.

Next, lower the belt all the way to its lowest point, and take another measurement. Only this time, measure the lowest point on the belt and add ³⁄₁₆ in. for clearance.

Now you can measure and mark for the motor-mount cutout. It's the same basic dance step. Measure from the center point on the back of the saw table to the top of the mount, subtracting a bit for clearance. To complete the layout, measure to the lower edge of the mount, adding the usual ³⁄₁₆-in. fudge factor.

Once all of the points have been marked on the plate, simply swing a compass to draw each of the arcs.

Next, mark where these arcs start (blade at 0°) and stop (blade at 45°). With the blade at 0°, measure from the left side of the saw to get end points for the belt and motor mount. You'll want to allow for clearance here, too. Then do the same with the blade at 45°.

One more thing. On my Delta, to allow the back plate to fit tightly against the back of the cabinet, I needed to make a cutout for the back end of the trunnion. It's just a bit more measuring and scribing with the compass. I also had to make a couple of straight clearance cuts to fit around the trunnion mounting bolts.

Once all of the arcs have been scribed, the top edge of the back plate can be trimmed even with the top end of the cabinet sides.

All that's left to do is cut out the marked openings with a sabersaw. But first drill ¾-in.-diameter holes at the corners of the openings. That way the corners end up with a nice radius.

After that, you can slip the plate into position on the back of the cabinet. You might have to loosen the bolts that mount the saw cabinet to the base so that you can raise the cabinet enough to get the plate in place. And to be able to mount the back to some saws, it's necessary to make a couple of horizontal cuts, so you end up attaching two pieces.

Check the clearance of the cutout by raising, lowering and pivoting the blade. If everything looks okay, go ahead and mount the plate to the back of the saw with a few sheet-metal screws. Once the back plate has been added, you can clamp the dust-collector hose to the port. Then turn on the dust collector, fire up the saw, and make some cuts. You'll notice a difference right away. More dust will be in the collector, where it belongs, than in the air you breathe.

DICK MCDONOUGH is a finish carpenter and wood-working teacher in Flint, Mich.

Sources

Woodworker's Supply
5604 Alameda Pl. NE
Albuquerque, NM 87113
Phone: 800-645-9292
www.woodworker.com

Shopmade Tablesaw Guards

BY
SANDOR NAGYSZALANCZY

"**B**lade guard removed for photo clarity." How many times have you been watching a home-improvement show or woodworking video and seen those words appear across the bottom of the television screen? Well, I want to know: what blade guard? In almost all the cases I've seen, a stock tablesaw guard wouldn't have worked in the applications shown.

What's a woodworker to do? Must we continually expose ourselves to unreason-

able risks when we perform operations that require removal of the tablesaw's standard blade guard—jobs like sawing tenons, cutting box joints, and cove cutting? I suppose we can hope our luck holds out, or we can wait for some kind of sensational all-purpose saw guard to hit the market. But I advocate another alternative: to design safer tablesaw jigs and setups by adding guards and safety devices that prevent accidental contact with the sawblade. I think any woodworker bright enough to design inno-

SAFETY WITHOUT SACRIFICE– A Plexiglas® shield keeps hands safely away from the blade without compromising visibility on the author's box-joint jig.

vative jigs for complicated woodworking tasks could make those same jigs a lot safer without investing too much extra time or material. After all, how much is a finger worth?

In this chapter, I'll show you some of my solutions for making common table-saw jigs and setups much safer. One thing I aim for in modifying my jigs is to reduce the degree to which safety relies on judgment. It's a given that, as you work, especially at repetitive tasks, there will be times when your attention flags or is diverted. A safe jig protects you during these lapses. The very best safety feature is one that eliminates the possibility of contacting the blade with anything but the stock. I try to get as close as possible to this ideal in all my jigs.

In many cases, I've retrofitted existing jigs with guards to show that you don't have to build all new devices to add safety to your woodworking. Because jigs are, by definition, custom-made, the safety measures you take will also have to be individualized. So I haven't tried to cover all the bases here, only to share a few specific solutions and underscore the general idea that safety and guarding features ought to be built into every jig you make.

Clear Guards for Sliding Jigs

Carriages that slide in the tablesaw's miter slots almost always require that the stock guard be removed. Whether you want to use a sliding crosscutting box or a jig for cutting tenons, dovetails, or box joints, you can easily retrofit clear blade guards that allow you to see what's going on but keep you from getting cut.

Box-joint-jig guard I made the guard for my box-joint jig shown in the photo on the facing page in about a half hour from a few scraps of wood and a Plexiglas cutoff purchased from a local plastics store. (Glass

REAR GUARD ACTION. The simple outrigger behind the box-joint jig lets you complete the cut without exposing the blade.

shops and hardware stores often carry clear plastic sheet goods.) The guard is a low box with wood sides and a Plexiglas top that mounts directly over the box-joint jig and provides protection ahead of and after the cut. As an added bonus, I noticed that it deflects chips and makes dust collection more efficient.

I made the guard's frame 21 in. wide by 10 in. long, which is wide enough to handle 10-in. drawer sides. I drilled holes in the ⅛-in.-thick Plexiglas sheet so that it could be screwed to the top of the frame (leave the protective paper on the Plexiglas during cutting and drilling to protect it from scratches). When attaching the plastic, I left it about an inch shy of the face of the jig, creating a slot for the workpiece. The 2-in.-high sides provide plenty of clearance between the plastic and the blade. I chamfered and waxed the lower edges of the sides to keep them gliding smoothly. Then I attached the guard to the back side of the box-joint jig with screws through the rear frame member.

To provide blade protection behind the jig, I added a second guard made from a block of wood and a 3-in. by 4-in. piece of Plexiglas, screwed to the underside of the rear frame member (see the photo above). Even if you don't want to make the entire

UNTOUCHABLE TENONING JIG.
An adjustable Plexiglas blade guard and a hand rest combine to keep your exposure to the blade near zero on this tenoning jig. The block that's clamped to the rip fence provides a positive stop and prevents the blade from cutting through the exit block at the back of the jig.

guard frame, adding a rear guard is an excellent idea. It protects you after the jig has been pushed through the cut when you're reaching over the saw table and are probably the most vulnerable to blade contact.

This type of exit guard is a good addition to any sliding jig. And you can make using it even safer by clamping a stop block to the rip fence or right to the table that will limit the forward travel of the jig—allowing a complete cut through the workpiece but stopping the blade short of the exit guard's rear block.

Tenoning-jig guard Protecting my hands from the blade involved the addition of three components to my sliding tenoning jig: a clear plastic shield ahead of the cut, an exit block to cover the blade behind the cut, and a hand rest to prevent my left hand, which holds the workpiece against the jig, from sliding down into harm's way, as shown in the photo above. The clear shield is nothing more than a 10-in.-long, 2½-in.-wide piece of ⅛-in.-thick Plexiglas screwed to the edge of a wood strip. This strip mounts to the face of the tenoning jig via

slotted holes I made using a straight bit in the plunge router. The slotted holes allow me to shift the shield in or out, depending on the width of the workpiece. I glued and screwed a 2½-in. by 2-in. by 1½-in. wood exit block to the back of the jig. I used a brass screw just in case it's accidentally hit by one of the two sawblades used during tenoning. A larger block would provide more protection, but as long as you use the jig in conjunction with a stop block, this size is fine. The final component, the hand rest, is a 4-in. by 2-in. by 1½-in. block glued to the edge of the tenoning jig's fence. You could position this block higher, if you find it more comfortable.

Crosscut-box guard A shopmade sliding crosscut box that rides in the tablesaw's miter slots is great for trimming and cross-cutting long boards or moldings. And adding a guard is the perfect way to make this sliding jig safer to use. The guard that I made for my crosscut box (see the top photo on the facing page) is basically an inverted U-shaped channel that rests on top of the stock over the line of cut, preventing hands from reaching into the blade. This design is very similar to the clear plastic guard that Kelly Mehler built in his article in *Fine Woodworking* #89, except that mine was made as a retrofit and has wood sides.

I started building the guard by cutting two 2¼-in.-wide, ⅜-in.-thick wood sides and a 3½-in.-wide, ⅛-in.-thick Plexiglas top, all slightly shorter than the front-to-back dimension inside my crosscut box. I then nailed sides and top together with #16 brass escutcheon pins through holes drilled in the plastic. Because the guard was retrofitted to my crosscut box, I couldn't cut grooves for the ends of the guard to slide in, as in Mehler's design. But for a smaller (12-in. capacity) box like mine, two narrow guide strips tacked on the inside of the box's front support are adequate to keep the guard in place and let it ride up and down.

Chamfering and rounding the ends and edges of the wood sides makes the guard slide up and down easily. To shield the blade where it exits the crosscut box, I added a rear guard that is a variation on the one for the box-joint jig described previously. In this case, I simply glued and screwed on a wood block to sheathe the blade.

Sliding miter-carriage guard Many woodworkers like to cut miters on the ends of moldings, picture frames, and other trim using a carriage with twin 45° fences, which slides in the tablesaw's miter-gauge slots. When you use this type of jig, you hold the workpiece against the fence during the cut, and your fingers often come close to the blade. And as you finish the cut, the blade exits between the fences, not far from where your thumbs are wrapped over the top of the fences. It's an operation that begs for a guard.

To add protection to my sliding miter jig (see lower photo at right), I cut a triangular block from some scrap 2x4 I had around the shop and glued and screwed it to the jig's baseplate just behind the intersection of the fences. This block acts as an exit guard and a mounting surface for a clear blade guard. The back end of this blade guard, a 5-in. by 12-in. piece of ⅛-in. Plexiglas, is screwed to the top of the block, and the front end is screwed to a wood strip nailed to the miter jig's front cross support. To complete the safety treatment, I clamp a stop block to the saw table to prevent the blade from cutting through the exit block.

Two Resawing Guards

Probably one of the most dangerous operations to perform on an unguarded tablesaw is resawing, for two reasons: First, the blade is usually raised to or near its full height. If there's a slipup, you are exposed to more

CROSSCUTS SAFE AND SIMPLE. **A three-sided box over the line of the cut reduces the chance of accidental blade contact on the author's crosscut jig. The box, with ⅜-in. wood sides and a ⅛-in. Plexiglas top, is held in place at one end by two cleats and rides up and down between them. An exit block guards the blade at the end of the cut.**

MITER SHIELD. **A triangular piece of 2x stock serves as an exit block as well as a mounting surface for the Plexiglas blade guard on this sliding miter-carriage jig.**

harm than with any other tablesaw operation. Second, there is maximum surface area contact between the wood and the blade. If the wood distorts and binds between the fence and blade (or the kerf closes up and pinches the blade), the workpiece is kicked back with the full force of the saw. These are two excellent reasons to invest a few minutes and a couple of pieces of wood to protect yourself against disaster.

I've come up with a pair of guarding devices for resawing. Both are simple, but effective. These jigs serve two purposes: They keep the board upright during the cut, and they keep your hands from coming anywhere near the blade.

The first is a clamp-on guard, as shown in the photo above. It consists of a 12-in.-long block of 4x4 lumber with a 2x2 stick screwed to one side. At 3½ in., the 4x4 is thicker than the depth of cut of most 10-in. tablesaws (if your sawblade rises higher, use a thicker block). The block is positioned over the throat plate, just far enough to the left of the blade to allow the stock to feed past. Because the resawn stock will have to be planed anyway, you can set the guard for

a fractionally loose fit to account for the distortion caused when the workpiece is cut. The 2x2 stick should be made long enough to center the 4x4 with respect to the blade arbor.

To use the clamp-on resaw guard, set the rip fence, lower the blade into the table, and put a piece of stock in place above the blade. Then position the block so it's over the throat plate and snugged up to the workpiece. Secure the end of the stick to the saw table with a C-clamp.

If you do a lot of resawing, you might want to make the second style of guard, which incorporates a dedicated throat plate. On this device, the wood block is attached directly to a replacement throat plate. In addition to providing protection like the clamp-on guard, this version enables you to raise the sawblade through the blank plate for a close fit that supports narrow workpieces right next to the blade. And it prevents the leading edge of the work from hanging up.

Make the replacement throat plate from plywood, particleboard, or Masonite that's the same thickness as the original plate. The easiest way I've found to shape the new plate is to use the factory throat plate as a template. I cut out a slightly oversize blank on the bandsaw, attach the factory plate to it with Scotch® brand 924 Adhesive Transfer Tape (available in ½ in. and ¾ in. widths), and then trim the new one to size using a piloted, flush-trimming router bit. Once the new plate fits snugly in your saw, screw on the block from below. I keep a couple of these dedicated throat plates handy—one for resawing 4/4 stock and one for 8/4. You can cut slots instead of holes for the screws through the replacement blank to permit adjustment for resawing boards of various thicknesses.

When working with either style of resaw guard, use a push stick to feed the end of the stock through the gap between block and fence—even if the blade is buried in the wood. If resawing must be done in two passes, set the blade height to slightly less than half the width of the board. The board is easily snapped apart after the second pass, and the small unsawn strip down the center of each resawn half can then be planed off. Incidentally, you can also use a similar guard—with a block that's not as high—when ripping narrow strips to width.

Hold-Down Cove-Cutting Guard

Passing your hands directly over the blade is dangerous. Even if the blade is buried in a thick workpiece, the stock might be kicked back, suddenly exposing the blade. In table-saw cove cutting, you have to keep constant downward pressure on the workpiece to get good results, so this danger is always present.

My cove-cutting guard (see the photo at right) is attached directly to a clamp-on fence, which guides the workpiece across the blade. The guard employs a featherboard-style hold-down over the blade. The hold-down prevents fingers from getting near the blade while keeping the stock flat on the table. And because the hold-down is firmly positioned, it does a better job of flattening the stock than your hands can. The only thing better than a guard like this is a power feeder, which will keep the stock flat on the table and your hands safely away from the blade while feeding the piece for you.

I made the cove-cutting fence from straight-grained stock; I used a 1¾-in.-wide, 1½-in.-thick piece of Douglas fir. A block of wood 1¾ in. by 3 in. by 4 in. is screwed to the top of this fence. Its position along the fence varies depending on the angle of the fence, which is determined by the desired cove profile. I cut the featherboard from a 4½-in.-long by 3-in.-wide by 2-in.-

thick block and cut the feathers on the bandsaw, making each one about ³⁄₃₂ in. thick. Then I attached the featherboard to the fence block with a ⅜-in.-diameter carriage bolt.

To use the device, clamp the fence to the saw table to the right of the sawblade with the guard centered over the blade. With the sawblade lowered into the table, place the workpiece under the featherboard. Pivot the featherboard until it exerts enough pressure on the piece to press it flat, but not so much that the workpiece is difficult to feed. Depending on the thickness of the work, you may have to relocate the hole for the carriage bolt in the fence block. Finally, clamp a secondary fence to the saw table to keep the work from wandering away from the main fence during cove cutting. As you make each pass over the blade (the blade should cut only about ¹⁄₁₆ in. deep each pass), use the next workpiece or a piece of scrapwood the same width as the workpiece to push the end of the work under the featherboard.

SANDOR NAGYSZALANCZY is the author of *Setting Up Shop, Workshop Dust Control* and *Tools: Rare and Ingenious* published The Taunton Press, Inc.

WIDE FEATHERBOARDS ARE EXCELLENT FOR COVING. They exert downward pressure over the cutting area while keeping hands from coming near the blade.

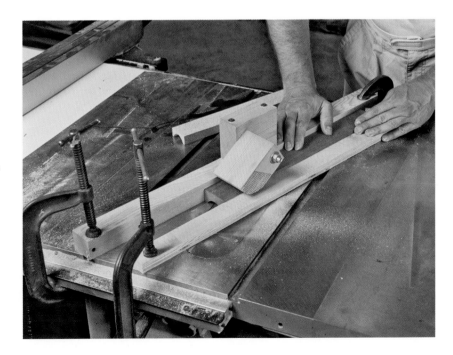

Causes and Prevention of Tablesaw Kickback

BY KELLY MEHLER

One afternoon, I was cutting a stack of walnut panels, about a foot square, on my tablesaw. I was being careful, but the repetitive work was mind numbing. My body was on autopilot, and my brain was taking a snooze. Then, wham! I was slammed in the gut, doubled over in front of the saw. There was no warning; I never saw it coming. It took a few seconds for me to realize that I had been hit by a piece of wood thrown off the tablesaw.

Later, in reconstructing what had happened, I guessed that a short piece of stock had pivoted into the back of the blade. The result was kickback.

Stock that's hurled by the tablesaw is pretty scary. I escaped serious injury, but I know others have not been so lucky. Recognizing the causes of kickback and its prevention is an important survival skill for any woodworker.

The potential for kickback is inherent with any circular saw, and on a tablesaw, kickback can occur when either ripping or crosscutting. Unlike a bandsaw, where the cutting force drives the stock into the table,

KICKBACK ZONE Teeth at the front of a tablesaw blade push stock down as they cut. But when the back of the blade comes into contact with the stock, it can be lifted off the table and thrown back violently at the operator.

Causes of Tablesaw Kickback

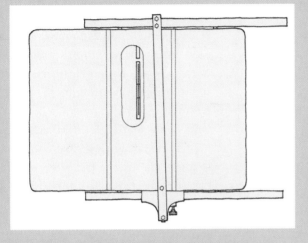

Misaligned fence forces stock into the back of the blade.

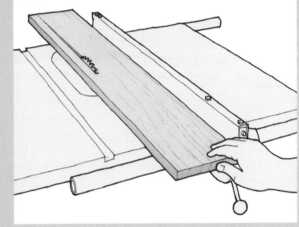

Stock with internal stress can pinch into the kickback zone.

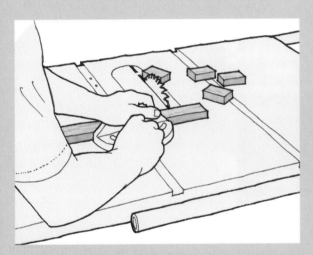

Small offcuts vibrate into the back of the blade.

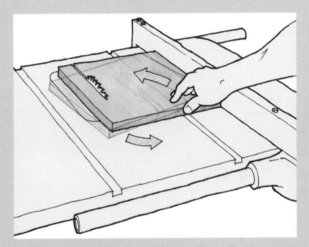

Short stock rotates into the kickback zone if not held tightly against the fence.

a tablesaw can lift the work off the table and throw it with tremendous force. Under normal conditions, teeth on the back of the blade, which are rising out of the table, don't encounter any resistance because they are in the kerf. Kickback results when stock comes into contact with the teeth at the back of the blade. With the outer edge of a typical 10-in. blade moving at about 100 mph, any workpiece can become a missile.

Even though tablesaw kickback is most commonly associated with ripping, it also can occur when you are crosscutting. Cut-off pieces that vibrate or are pushed into the back of the blade can be launched toward the operator.

A Good Splitter

Preventing the workpiece from contacting the back of the blade is the only foolproof solution to kickback. This is the job of the splitter. A blade guard alone does not work.

Most stock tablesaw splitters are part of a three-in-one unit (see the photo below), which includes a blade guard, anti-kickback pawls, and a splitter. When installed and aligned, this kind of splitter works well for ripping stock. But it must be removed from the saw when cutting grooves and tenon shoulders and when the stock is not cut completely through. The splitter tilts with the trunnion, but it doesn't rise and fall as blade height is adjusted, so the lower the blade is set, the greater the gap from the back of the blade to the splitter. Consequently, with typical ¾-in.-thick stock, there is a gap of about 2 in. between the back of

the blade and the splitter. Kickback can occur before the work reaches the splitter.

Another splitter, like the one in the top left photo on the facing page, has anti-kickback pawls and is used with a separate blade guard. It mounts to the saw's trunnion and shares the same shortcomings as the three-in-one unit. The real advantage of this design is that it dismounts and remounts quickly, eliminating one of the chief complaints with the other design.

The best design, one that comes closest to totally eliminating kickback, is the splitter that rises and falls with the blade (see the top right photo on the facing page). As far as I know, this splitter is available only on some European tablesaws. Because it attaches to the arbor assembly, it can be set close to the blade teeth and below the top of the blade. This is handy because the splitter does not have to be removed when stock isn't cut all the way through.

A throat plate–mounted splitter is another option. It's a thin, hardwood fin glued into a shopmade, wooden throat plate just behind the blade. Because this splitter does not rise or tilt, you may have to make several of them, so you have one suited to the stock thickness you're working with.

Other Precautions

Besides a good splitter, other commercial and shop-built fixtures can help prevent kickback. Your strongest allies may be care and common sense. The tablesaw is an easy tool to take for granted, especially when you're tired or in a hurry.

Equipment you can buy or make A fence that angles toward the blade encourages kickback, so make sure the fence is parallel to the blade or angled away from it slightly. For crosscutting, a crosscut box or a fence attached to the miter gauge keeps cutoffs

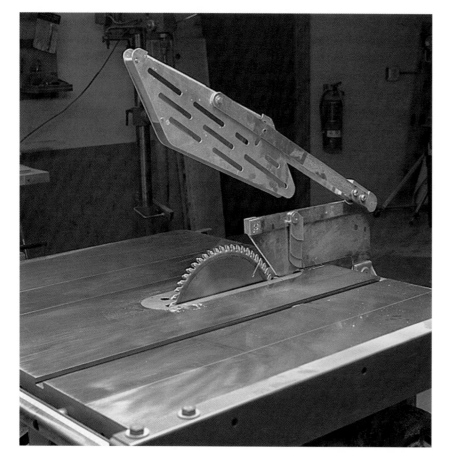

A SPLITTER HELPS PREVENT KICKBACK. This one, with anti-kickback pawls and a guard, must be removed when not cutting completely through the stock.

GOOD SPLITTER. **This splitter is more likely to be used because it dismounts and remounts easily.**

BEST SPLITTER. **This one closely hugs the back of the blade and can be left in place for all cutting operations.**

away from the blade (see the bottom right photo on p. 112).

A well-designed push stick is a must for keeping your hand out of danger. A good push stick holds down the work on the saw's table and allows you to steer the work against the fence (see the left photo on p.112). The type that I prefer is shaped like a shoe and is much better than a stick with a bird's mouth in the end.

There are several types of fence-mounted, anti-kickback wheels (see the bottom photo at right), but they all operate on the same principle. The wheels allow rotation only in the feed direction, and they lock when the stock is pushed toward the operator. The wheels are angled so that they force stock against the rip fence.

A featherboard clamped to a table is a low-tech but effective way of preventing kickback (see the top right photo on p. 112). The featherboard has a series of closely spaced kerfs cut into one end. The spring-like fingers hold the work tightly against the

ANTI-KICKBACK WHEELS. **These wheels drive the stock against the fence.**

fence, and they act like a pawl to prevent the stock from being pushed backward.

Shop practices help, too. A sharp blade cuts with less resistance, reducing the chances of kickback, so it's a good idea to check your blade regularly. Don't stand directly in line with the blade. By standing off to the side, you'll be out of the way if the blade catches a piece of stock and throws it. And it pays to know when to quit. When you're tired or when someone breaks your concentration, it's time to turn off the machine. Kickback happens instantly and seldom when you're expecting it.

KELLY MEHLER, of Berea, Ky., is a professional furni-turemaker and the author of *The Table Saw Book* (2003), published by The Taunton Press, Inc.

PUSH STICK. **A large push stick keeps the stock against the fence and holds it on the table. Note that the author is not standing in line with the blade.**

FEATHERBOARD. **A featherboard holds the stock against the fence, reducing the chance of kickback. Mount the featherboard in front of the blade.**

MITER GAUGE. **A miter-gauge fence prevents kickback by pushing off-cuts away from the blade and providing more support to the stock.**

Tablesaw Kickback

On the first day of class, I ask my woodworking students if they've had a kickback on the tablesaw. I always get a fair number of hands in the air, but few of the students can tell me what happened. And often those who have had the unsettling experience of carving a nice, deep furrow in a piece of wood and having it fly across the shop don't usually know what caused it. It all happens so fast that it's over by the time they realize it's occurred.

Before I let my students get near a tablesaw, I do a little dog-and-pony show to demonstrate the dangers of kickback. Using

BY LON SCHLEINING

A Shopmade Splitter
BY KELLY MEHLER

Most woodworkers understand the importance of a zero-clearance insert and either buy blanks or make their own. To add a splitter to one of these inserts, I just glue a piece of wood into the slot behind the blade. The splitter stock should be the same thickness as the blade and should fit in the mating slot the raised blade cuts in the throat plate. The splitter is most effective when it is placed closest to the back of the blade. Because the blade progresses toward the back of the insert as it is raised for thicker cuts, I suggest at least two inserts—one for cutting thin stock, up to about 1 in. and another for thick stock.

To make an insert for thick stock, you must elongate the slot by flipping the insert end for end and then raising the blade. This allows you to place the splitter farther back on the insert. I always drill a finger hole in the insert for easy removal. A short adjustment screw can be embedded into the side and/or end of the insert to take up any play in the fit, and the splitter can be sanded.

The important thing is to align the right edge of the splitter with the right side of the blade (the side closest to the fence).

SIMPLE BUT SAFE. A splitter is essential to any safe shop, but it doesn't have to cost a thing. Flip a zero-clearance insert end for end and raise the blade to elongate the slot. Fit a piece of hardwood tightly into the slot and then glue it in place.

This keeps the workpiece against the fence for a smoother cut. Also, it virtually eliminates the chance of kickback.

I make the splitter by slicing a piece of hardwood and trimming it until I get a tight fit in the slot. Then I glue it in place. I make my splitters out of hardwood, but there is no reason why they could not be made of aluminum, plastic or any other durable material.

KELLY MEHLER is a woodworker in Berea, Ky., and the author of *The Table Saw Book* (2003), published by The Taunton Press, Inc.

In a Blink of an Eye, You Have Trouble

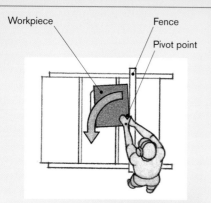

Workpiece — Fence — Pivot point

1, 2 The author stands in a normal position to begin the cut, but for demonstration purposes, he moves out of the way before allowing the workpiece to kick back. Do not try this yourself.

3, 4 As the piece veers slightly away from the fence, it binds up between the fence and the blade. Though the gap between the fence and the piece is too small for the camera to pick up, it is enough to cause plenty of trouble. The back of the blade lifts the piece off the table, with the back corner of the piece (against the fence and closest to the operator) acting as a pivot point.

5 The piece rides across the spinning blade and is catapulted into the air.

  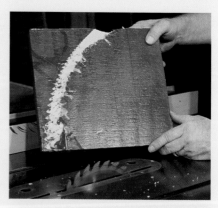

6, 7 With a few horsepower of force behind it, the piece bullets across the room until it crashes into something. The author would have risked being hit had he stood where an operator normally stands.

8 The crescent shape on a piece that kicks back is the result of the piece riding across the top of the spinning blade. Using a splitter almost eliminates the chance of this happening.

Styrofoam® to represent a piece of plywood, I show how the cut should be made and then what occurs if the piece drifts away from the rip fence. Crouching out of the flight path, I simply let go of the piece for a second, and off it goes.

A kickback occurs when the leading corner of a piece being cut rotates away from the rip fence. The piece then gets caught up between the back of the blade and the fence. As the back of the blade—the part that cuts upward—begins to gnaw into the freshly cut edge of the piece, the piece quickly rotates, getting caught diagonally between the fence and the blade. The corner of the piece closest to the operator and against the rip fence is the pivot point around which a radius cut is made. The piece then acts like a pole-vaulter. Rotating further and moving faster now, the piece rides up and over the blade and is hurtled into the air to the left side of the blade. If you're lucky, it will fly over your left shoulder. If you're not lucky, a board with a few horsepower of force behind it will hit you. This is also why it is such a bad idea to stand to the left of the operator and watch him work.

Afterward, you'll usually spot a crescent-shaped cut on the bottom of the piece. This crescent cut is the result of the piece rotating as it crosses over the top of the blade. It's as if you drew a circle with a compass, putting the center point at the corner closest to the operator and against the fence.

Certain types of cuts are more prone to kickback than others. A square piece being trimmed is the most likely to cause trouble, because any drift away from the fence will cause the piece to bind. Any piece cut against the rip fence that is either square or rectangular (with a width approaching at least half or more of its length) is a very hazardous cut. Typically, troublesome pieces are drawer bottoms and small parts.

But if the piece is kept solidly against the rip fence and pushed all the way through the cut and beyond the blade, it's unlikely that a kickback will occur. Keep your eyes on the rip fence just past the blade to make sure the piece is firmly in contact with the fence throughout the cut. The critical time is often just after the front of the blade has cut all the way through the piece. The waste lies on the table rattling against the blade, distracting you from the very real task of keeping the piece firmly against the rip fence until it is well past the blade. A moment's inattention and…

After the class understands the danger of kickback, I repeat the operation with the splitter and blade guard in place. When I let go this time, nothing happens. Then I use a push stick to force the piece away from the rip fence and into the blade. Again, nothing happens. This is because the splitter prevents the rotation of the piece away from the fence.

Kickbacks can be prevented. They are virtually impossible with an anti-kickback splitter in place. The splitter keeps the stock solidly against the rip fence and prevents any rotation toward the blade. Without this rotation, kickback is virtually unheard of. Use the splitter that came with your saw, buy an after-market splitter, or make one yourself, but don't make cuts on the tablesaw without one.

LON SCHLEINING is a woodworker in Dana Point, Calif. He is the author of *Treasure Chests* (2001) and *The Workbench* (2004), both published by The Taunton Press, Inc.

Reproducing Your Project

BY KEN PICOU

You've just built a piece of furniture that you really like, and you know that you'll want to build it again. It might be a personal project, or if you're a professional woodworker, maybe it's a design that you'd like to produce regularly or as commissions arise. Many projects—especially chairs—can be quite confusing because of all the components and all the angles that need to be accu-rately cut. Once you've done the thinking and gone through the whole trial-and-error process, so everything's set up and working well, why not record all the necessary information, so you can reproduce your design simply and accurately anytime you wish with very little setup time?

Faced with the economic reality of woodworking as a profession, I came up with a simple system for duplicating

THE AUTHOR'S CHAIRS, in mesquite and in bird's-eye maple, are comfortable, handsome and relatively straightforward to make with his production techniques.

furniture parts without spending a great deal of time setting up or having to remember just what it was I did last time. My system is based on the use of two easily made items: a sliding crosscut box dedicated to the design in question and a set of templates, which I use in conjunction with a bearing-guided, flush-trimming drum sander for shaping any curved parts. With these two tools, I'm able to produce my

side chair (see the photo on the facing page) in about 12 hours, from dimensioned lumber to finished chair. The technique can be used for any piece of furniture and works fine regardless of how many angles or curves are in a piece. Here's how I do it.

A Dedicated Crosscut Box

The dedicated crosscut box starts as a basic shopmade crosscut box with runners to fit in

ATTACH THE TEMPLATE. Screws connecting template and stock are all positioned so they fall in mortises, in waste stock, or beyond where a piece will be crosscut to final length. The section of the template that extends past the notches indicating the end of the chair leg provides a reference surface to position the leg squarely in a router jig for mortising.

TEMPLATE SANDING. With the template attached to its underside, a front chair rail is easily sanded to shape using the author's invention, the Robo-Sander, which is a bearing-guided sanding drum. Using the drum instead of a bearing-guided router bit prevents tearout, especially in heavily figured woods such as this bird's-eye maple.

the saw table's miter-gauge slots. I then add a removable pivoting fence for cutting angled parts. All stops and angles for a project are marked on the table along with the name of the part and the width of stock (see the photo on the facing page). If I need to cut an extra-long piece, I just screw a story pole to the table (or to the pivoting fence) and clamp my stock to the story pole. I use a small, wooden handscrew as a stop whenever I'm doing more than a few like items. I set the stop so it's about ¼ in. above the table, which allows sawdust to escape rather than getting stuck between my stock and stop, throwing off my measurement.

Templates and Template Sanding

After I've cut all my blanks using the dedicated crosscut box, I use my templates as patterns (see the photo on p. 117) and mark the blanks for rough cutting on the bandsaw. I use phenolic-resin board for my templates because the material will stand up indefinitely. If your templates won't be seeing a

THE DEDICATED CROSSCUT BOX. This box lets the author make virtually identical copies of his design next week, next year, or in 10 years. All angles, stock widths, part names, and cutoff points are marked on the box, making production a simple matter of running through the cut list.

lot of use, cabinet-grade plywood will work fine.

I bandsaw out the parts and screw the templates to their respective parts, keeping the screw holes in waste material or where there will be a mortise (see the top photo on the facing page). Then I template-sand the parts to shape with a bearing-guided, flush-trimming drum sander I designed for this purpose, as shown in the bottom photo on the facing page. You could also use a bearing-guided, flush-trimming router bit, but in highly figured stock—such as bird's-eye maple—tearout is almost inevitable.

It pays to take your time and get the template exactly the way you want the part to be. Often, you can use the original part (from a prototype) to make the template by attaching the rough-cut template stock to the original part with double-sided tape and template-sanding the template.

I usually run my sander with a 50-grit sleeve at 1,700 rpm to 1,800 rpm. I've found this to be a good combination to remove stock quickly without burning the

wood. I use a ¾-in. plywood subtable on my drill press when I'm template-sanding because it allows me to adjust the height of my sander's phenolic-resin bearing. I drill a recess hole for the bearing, making it ¼ in. oversize to prevent any binding. Being able to adjust the bearing vertically so that its top is just flush with the top of the template ensures that the drum is removing stock evenly over the entire width of my blank. Also, the recess in the subtable allows me to run the bearing all the way below the subtable's surface. Thus I can use the drum freehand in case I need to do any touch-up work. The sanding drum can also be used as a vertical thickness sander when used with a one-point vertical fence. I find this useful when thicknessing chair backrests.

KEN PICOU is a designer and woodworker in Austin, Tex.

Making a Sliding Saw Table

BY GUY PEREZ

A SLIDING TABLE IMPROVES CROSSCUTTING AND MITERING. Guy Perez made this sliding table to extend the usefulness of his old Sears contractor's saw. Using lightweight everyday construction materials like plywood, pine and aluminum angle, Perez built the table with an adjustable fence, which makes the jig ideal for multiple crosscutting and for mitering.

Until I came upon a 9-in., used tablesaw (a 1937 Craftsman model), I cut all my wood with an 8¼-in. circular saw aligned by a pair of shopmade guides. But even the Sears® tablesaw still lacked a stand, table extensions, and a miter gauge. So I set out to bring my bargain saw up to a higher standard.

The first additions I made to the saw included a stand, table extensions, and a T-square fence, which allows me to rip stock up to 32 in. wide. These improvements served me well through several furniture projects, but I continued to crosscut with my circular saw and guide instead of using a miter gauge. As I saw it, standard miter gauges have three weaknesses: Their bars often fit loosely in the miter slots, they don't support long pieces well, and they're ineffective for crosscutting wide pieces, especially sheet stock. I decided a sliding table would solve all of those problems.

But I found that most commercial sliding tables cost in excess of $350. The ones I looked at also failed to address another constraint I had—scarcity of shop space. So I built a scaled-down sliding table (see the photo at left) that has a 32-in. crosscut capacity. The table cost me less than $100, but it performs comparably to the expensive commercial models. It was fairly easy to build, too, and I can still roll my entire tablesaw out of the way to save space.

How the Table Slides

Like a few of its store-bought cousins, my sliding table rolls on precision bearings that are guided by steel rails. The whole assembly consists of four main components: an 18-in. by 24-in. plywood table, an 18-in.-long carriage that has four pairs of bearings, two 5-ft.-long tubular guide rails and a 60-in.-

long aluminum crosscutting fence. Similar to one of Robland's sliding tables, the rails are spaced about 6 in. apart and are mounted left of the saw table. Detail A on p. 122 shows the wooden frame I built to support the rails. You can easily modify the frame to suit the saw you have, as long as the sliding table is level with and travels parallel to the saw table.

Constructing the Table

Before you start to build a sliding table, there are a couple of things worth noting about aluminum. First, when buying aluminum bar or angle, check out recycling centers and salvage yards because they usually don't require a minimum quantity or charge the premium that metal-supply shops often do. Second, you can cut aluminum to length on a table-saw fitted with a carbide-tipped blade. But be sure you don't let the hot chips touch your skin.

Carriage The carriage is the heart of the sliding table, so I built it first. It acts much like a sliding dovetail joint, in which a pin is held by the tapered dovetail groove, thus restricting side-to-side or up-and-down movement. In my sliding table, the pin is replaced by guide rails captured by opposing pairs of bearings. By mounting the bearings 45° above and below the plane of the rails, I restricted both lateral and vertical carriage motion while allowing the table to roll forward and back.

I mounted two pairs of bearings and spacers to each of two bearing brackets (¾-in.- by 18-in.-long aluminum angles), putting one bearing and spacer pair at each end (see the bottom photo at right). The bearings and spacers I used are intended for skateboard wheels and are available at most sporting-goods stores and hobby shops for around $16 for eight bearings with spacers. I secured each bearing bracket to the vertical leg of the side brackets (1½-in.- by 14-in.-long aluminum angles) so that each leg of the bearing-bracket angle is 45° off

THE GUIDE SYSTEM IS STRONG AND ACCURATE. **Adapting a design from commercial-grade sliding tables, Perez made a skateboard-bearing carriage and attached it to the underside of the table. The carriage is guided by a pair of tubular rails.**

CROSSCUTTING FENCE, EXTENSION AND OUTFEED TABLES. **These parts add to the accuracy, safety, and versatility of the author's saw. Reduced friction and vibration of the sliding table are real assets when crosscutting long stock and sheet goods or mitering pieces–operations made possible by the added accessories.**

the horizontal plane of the rails. I found it easiest to first drill the mounting holes in the 1½-in. side-bracket angles. Then, with the ¾-in. bearing-bracket angle clamped in place, I drilled its corresponding holes.

The side-to-bearing-bracket assemblies are held together by two tension rods (I used hex bolts, but ⅜-in. threaded rod will also do). The tension rods allow the carriage to be precisely fit to the guide rails. The rods are fastened so that they turn freely in a mounting plate and are fixed to another plate with a T-nut that's epoxied in place. The 1⅛-in.-thick hardwood

Sliding Table Anatomy

The sliding table attaches to a carriage, which has bearings that ride along tubular guide rails (see Detail C). The rails are mounted to a frame that's fastened to the saw's stand (see Detail A). Because the fence (Detail B) pivots, the sliding table can easily crosscut and miter both sheet goods and long stock.

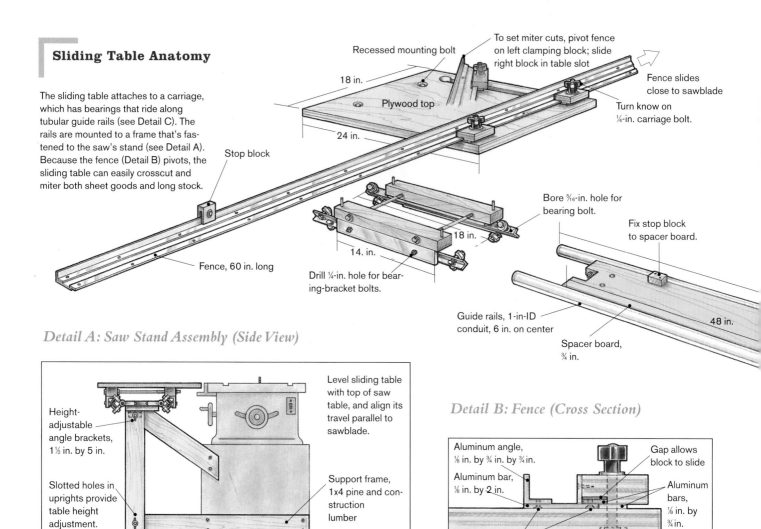

To set miter cuts, pivot fence on left clamping block; slide right block in table slot

Recessed mounting bolt

18 in.

Plywood top

24 in.

Stop block

Fence slides close to sawblade

Turn know on ¼-in. carriage bolt.

Fence, 60 in. long

18 in.

14. in.

Drill ¼-in. hole for bearing-bracket bolts.

Bore ⁵⁄₁₆-in. hole for bearing bolt.

Fix stop block to spacer board.

Guide rails, 1-in-ID conduit, 6 in. on center

Spacer board, ¾ in.

48 in.

Detail A: Saw Stand Assembly (Side View)

Height-adjustable angle brackets, 1½ in. by 5 in.

Slotted holes in uprights provide table height adjustment.

Level sliding table with top of saw table, and align its travel parallel to sawblade.

Support frame, 1x4 pine and construction lumber

Detail B: Fence (Cross Section)

Aluminum angle, ⅛ in. by ¾ in. by ¾ in.

Aluminum bar, ⅛ in. by 2 in.

Gap allows block to slide

Aluminum bars, ⅛ in. by ¾ in.

⅛-in. pop rivits, 6-in. on center

---

mounting plates are screwed to the top of each 1½-in. angle. Four T-nuts with bolts near the ends of the mounting plates secure the table to the carriage.

Guide-rail assembly I built the guide-rail system to fit between the four pairs of carriage bearings. For the rails, I used 1-in. ID electrical conduit, which goes for about $4 per 10 ft. at building supply stores. I bolted a 6-in.-wide strip of ¾-in. particleboard as a spacer between the rails to stiffen them and keep them parallel. An easy way to determine the exact width of the spacer board is to set the tension rods, so there is ½ in. of adjustment either way. Then hold the rails between the bearings, and measure the distance between the rails. Because the spacer

board is cove cut on both edges to accept the tubing, add ¼ in. to the measurement. In each of the rails, I cut three keyhole-shaped slots by drilling sets of holes—each set with a ½-in. hole overlapping a ¼-in. hole. The slots let me insert the hex bolts that fix the rails to the spacer board. I screwed a block at the rear of the spacer board to limit the table's travel. Then I added a turn block at the front (see the top photo on p. 121), which lets me release the carriage from the guide rails.

Support frame To make the frame that supports the guide-rail system, I used eight board feet of 1x4 pine. I made the frame so I could easily get to all my saw's controls. Two 1½-in.- by 5-in.-long aluminum-angle

Detail C: Carriage Assembly (End View)

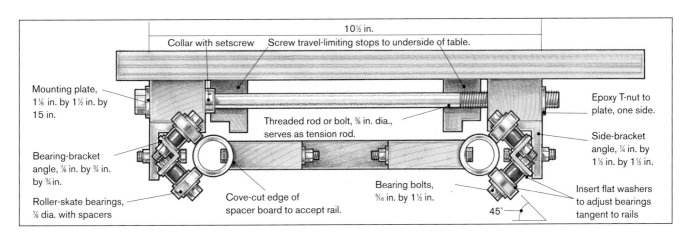

10½ in.

Collar with setscrew   Screw travel-limiting stops to underside of table.

Mounting plate,
1⅛ in. by 1½ in. by
15 in.

Threaded rod or bolt, ⅜ in. dia.,
serves as tension rod.

Epoxy T-nut to
plate, one side.

Bearing-bracket
angle, ⅛ in. by ¾ in.
by ¾ in.

Side-bracket
angle, ¼ in. by
1½ in. by 1½ in.

Roller-skate bearings,
⅞ dia. with spacers

Cove-cut edge of
spacer board to accept rail.

Bearing bolts,
⁵⁄₁₆ in. by 1½ in.

Insert flat washers
to adjust bearings
tangent to rails

45°

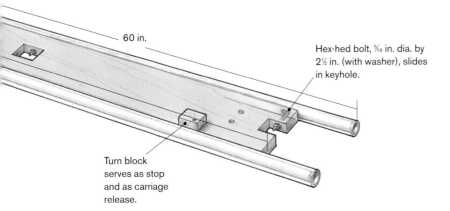

60 in.

Hex-hed bolt, ⁵⁄₁₆ in. dia. by
2½ in. (with washer), slides
in keyhole.

Turn block
serves as stop
and as carriage
release.

brackets hold the assembly to the frame's uprights. Slotted holes in the uprights and oversize holes in the brackets provide the means for height adjustment.

Final Adjustments

The carriage should be fit to the guide rails before you mount the sliding top. After adjusting the tension bolts so the bearings fit the rails, you should check two other things to ensure that the table will slide properly. First, the bearings should contact each guide rail tangentially. Second, each mounting plate should be parallel to the rail below it. I adjusted my bearings by using flat washers to get the proper spacing. To ensure parallel travel (vertically with respect to the rails), I used a combination square and set each mounting plate the same distance above the rails at the front and rear. Initially, my carriage was misaligned. To fix this, I elongated the

bearing-to-side-bracket holes using a rat-tail file, and then I repositioned the brackets.

I made the final carriage adjustments with the sliding table in place. To align the sliding table with the top of the saw table, I clamped 4-ft.-long straightedges across the front and rear of the saw table. I leveled the sliding table up to the straightedges and tightened the frame's height-adjustment bolts. Next, I clamped a board to the sliding table, perpendicular to the rails. I drove a finishing nail in one end of the board, leaving it about ¼ in. proud. As I moved the table to and fro (with the saw unplugged), I measured from the nail head to the blade, both front and back. Once I was sure the table was parallel, I snugged up all the mounting bolts. Then I screwed travel-limiting stops to the underside of the table in line with the spacer-board blocks. To position the stop blocks, I rolled the carriage and marked limits for the table's normal movement.

Finally, I equipped my sliding table with a 60-in. crosscut fence. Because the fence is adjustable, I can set it for mitering, and I can position it to support a workpiece right up to the blade. Fitted with an adjustable stop, my fence and sliding table made quick work of cutting the slats for a crib and a couch I was building.

★Please note price estimates are from 1993.

GUY PEREZ is a woodworker in Madison, Wisc.

One-Stop Cutting Station

BY KEN PICOU

Tablesaws are excellent for ripping stock, but the standard miter gauge that comes with most tablesaws makes them mediocre at best for cross-cutting material or cutting joinery. But by making a simple sliding-crosscut box and a few accessory jigs, you can greatly increase the accuracy and flexibility of your saw and turn it into a one-stop cutting station, capable of crosscutting, tenoning and slotting.

The system I've developed consists of a basic sliding-crosscut box with a 90° back rail, a removable pivoting fence, a tenoning attachment, and a corner slotting jig, for cutting the slots for keyed miter joints (see the photo below). This system is inherently safer and more accurate than even the most expensive miter gauge for several reasons. First, it uses both miter slots, so there is less side play than with a miter gauge. Second,

MAKING A CROSSCUT BOX MORE VERSATILE. An accurate sliding-crosscut box makes a good base for cutting accessories, including this corner-slotting jig. This jig mounts or dismounts in seconds and makes for strong miter joints in picture or mirror frames and in small boxes or drawers.

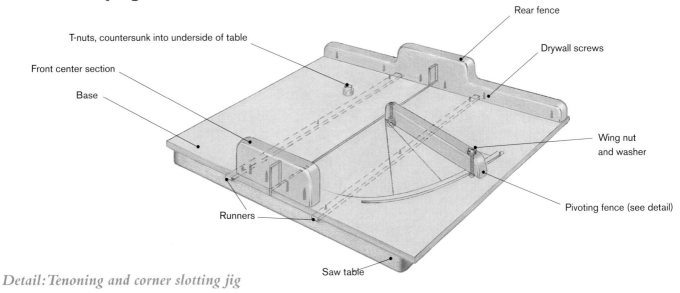

Rear fence

T-nuts, countersunk into underside of table

Drywall screws

Front center section

Base

Wing nut
and washer

Pivoting fence (see detail)

Runners

Saw table

Detail: Tenoning and corner slotting jig

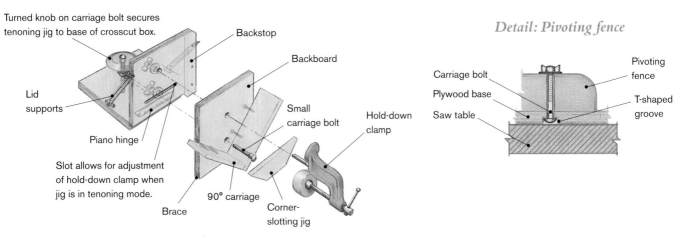

Turned knob on carriage bolt secures
tenoning jig to base of crosscut box.

Backstop

Backboard

Lid
supports

Small
carriage bolt

Hold-down
clamp

Piano hinge

Slot allows for adjustment
of hold-down clamp when
jig is in tenoning mode.

90° carriage

Corner-
slotting jig

Brace

Detail: Pivoting fence

Pivoting
fence

Carriage bolt

Plywood base

Saw table

T-shaped
groove

the work slides on a moving base, so there's no chance of the work slipping or catching from friction with the saw table. Third, the long back fence provides better support than a miter gauge, which is usually only 4 in. or 5 in. across. Fourth, the sliding-crosscut box is big, so angles can be measured and divided much more accurately than with a miter gauge (the farther from its point of origin an angle is measured, the greater the precision). Finally, the sliding crosscut box is a stable base on which to mount various attachments, such as a tenoning jig or a corner slotting jig, which can greatly expand the versatility of the tablesaw.

Building the Basic Crosscut Box

I cut the base of my sliding-crosscut box from a nice, flat sheet of ½-in.-thick Baltic birch plywood, and then I make it a little bit wider and deeper than my saw's table-top. A cheaper grade of plywood also would be fine for this jig, but I decided to use a premium material because I wanted the jig to be a permanent addition to my shop.

The runners that slide in the tablesaw's miter-gauge slots can be made from any stable material that wears well. I prefer wood to metal because wood works easily, and I can screw right into it. I usually use hard maple, and I've never had a problem.

ACCURATE HOLES ARE KEY TO AN ACCURATE JIG. **Clamps hold the crosscut-box runners in place while the author drills and screws the runners to the base. Using a Vix (self-centering) bit in the previously drilled and countersunk holes in the runner keeps the bit centered going into the plywood, which helps keep the screws from pulling the runners out of line.**

CHECKING AND RECHECKING FOR A PERFECT 90°. **Measuring with a square and making test cuts is time well spent. The accuracy of the whole crosscut box and all jigs that mount to it depends on getting the relationship of rear fence to blade just right.**

Using a long-wearing, slippery plastic such as an acetal (Delrin®, for example) or ultra-high molecular-weight (UHMW) plastic is also a possibility.

I start with a maple board of sufficient length that is at least as wide as three or four runners are thick. I plane this board, taking off minute increments with each pass, until it slides easily on edge in one of the slots but isn't sloppy. Once the fit's right, I rip the runners from this board, setting the fence on my tablesaw to just under the depth of the miter-gauge slot. Then I drill and counter-sink them at the middle and near both ends (I check the dimensions of the Baltic birch base to make sure I drill the screw holes so they'll fall near the edges of the base). I usu-ally drill a couple of holes near each end as insurance in case a screw drifts off when I'm screwing the runners to the base.

Next, I crank the sawblade all the way down below the table and lay the runners in the miter-gauge slots. I position the base so that its back edge is parallel to the rear of the saw table and the front edge overhangs by a couple of inches. I clamp the runners to the base in the front. I drill pilot holes in the plywood from below using a Vix bit (a self-

centering drill bit available through most large tool catalogs) placed in one of the countersunk holes in the runners. Then I screw up through the runners into the base. When I've done both runners at the front of the saw, I slide the base back carefully and repeat at the rear (see the left photo above). I check for binding or wobble by sliding the base back and forth a few times. If the fit is less than ideal, I still have four more chances (the extra screw holes I drilled at both ends of each runner) to get it right. If the fit is good, I drill pilot holes with the Vix bit and screw the runner to the base in the middle, taking care not to let the runner move side to side. I also trim the runners flush with the front and back of the crosscut box.

If the fit's a bit too snug at first, use will tend to burnish the runners so that they will glide more easily. If, after some use they're still a little snug, you can sand the runners just a bit and give them a coat of paste wax. That will usually get them gliding nicely.

Building accuracy into the jig An inaccu-rate jig is useless, so it's essential that assem-bly of this jig be dead-on. Fortunately, this isn't difficult; it just takes a little time and patience.

I made both the back fence and the front center section from straight-grained red oak, but any straight-grained hardwood will do (see the drawing on p. 125). I make sure the center portions of both pieces are built up high enough to provide 1½-in. clearance with the blade cranked up all the way.

The front section helps keep the table flat and prevents it from being sawn in half. Because this front section is not a reference surface, its position isn't critical, so I screw it on first.

Then I mount the rear fence about ¼ in. in from and parallel to the back of the Baltic birch base. I clamp the fence to the base and drive one screw through the base, which I've already drilled and countersunk, into the fence a couple of inches to the right of where the blade will run. This provides a pivot point, making it easier to align the rear fence to the blade.

I remove the clamp, raise the blade up through the base and cut through the front section and the base, staying just shy of the rear fence. So far, there's only one screw holding the rear fence in place. To set the rear fence permanently and accurately at 90° to the blade, I place the long leg of a framing square against the freshly made kerf (saw is off) and the short leg against the fence. With the fence flush against the square, I clamp the fence on an overhanging edge and do a test cut on a wide piece of scrap. I check this for square with a combination square and adjust the position of the fence as necessary. When I've got it right, I put another clamp on the fence near the blade on the side opposite my one screw. Then I drill, countersink and screw through the base into the fence right next to the clamp, and I check the fence's position again to make sure screwing it to the base didn't pull it off the mark (see the right photo on the facing page). I also make another test cut, and as long as it's still good, I screw the fence down near the ends and the middles

on both sides of the blade (see the drawing on p. 125). If the second cut is not a perfect 90°, then I'll fiddle with the fence until the cut is perfect before screwing it into position permanently. Time spent getting the fence right is time well spent. If, for aesthetic reasons, you want the rear of the base to be flush with the fence, you can trim the base flush with a bearing-guided, flush-trimming router bit. Either way, the performance of the crosscut box will be unaffected.

Anything from a small wooden hand-screw to a fancy commercially made stop will work as a stop block for this fence. A self-stick ruler can be added to the fence or table.

REAR FENCE HELPS ALIGN JIG'S HINGE. **Using the rear fence as his reference, the author aligns the tenoning jig's hinge with a square. The Vix bit ensures that the screw holes are centered, so the screws will go in true and the hinge will be straight.**

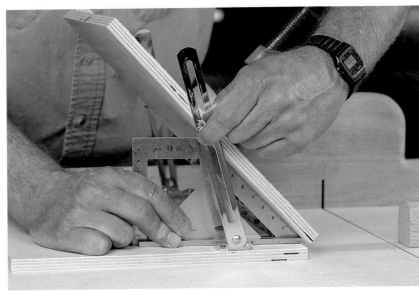

GET THE ANGLE RIGHT. **Setting angles accurately can be done quickly with a miter square or a bevel square. By setting the angle both fore and aft in the tenoning jig, you can be sure the angle will be true across the face of the jig.**

QUICK, ACCURATE TENONS.
It's easy to cut tenons with the author's hinged jig. A hold-down clamp grabs the workpiece securely and accommodates almost any size workpiece. The big footprint of the tenoning jig's base anchors it securely to the base of the crosscut jig below. The jig is also useful for cutting long miters and angled tenons.

A Pivoting Fence

I wanted a pivoting fence for making angled cuts, but I also wanted to be able to remove the fence quickly when I need to cut wide boards. I accomplished this first by setting a T-nut for the pivot point into the underside of the jig's base about 6 in. forward of the fixed fence. Then I routed an arc-shaped track for a carriage bolt at the end of the fence (see the drawing on p. 125). The arc runs from 0° to a bit more than 45°, and there's a plunge-routed hole just below the 0° point through which the carriage-bolt assembly can be lifted out to remove the fence. I marked two common angles (22½° and 45°) onto the jig for quick reference using a large protractor and transferring that angle to a bevel square and then to the plywood. These angles can also be checked and fine-tuned by cutting them, setting the resulting blocks together and checking for 90° with an accurate square.

A slotted screw and washer secure the fence at its pivot point but allow the fence to move, and a wing nut (with washer) fixes the angle of the fence at its outboard end. As with the fixed fence, a stop block may be as simple or sophisticated as you like.

An Adjustable Tenoning Jig

A simple hinged jig that uses the rear fence as a reference surface will allow you to cut both regular and angled tenons, rabbets and angled edges accurately and without too much fuss. I built this jig also from Baltic birch plywood. I crosscut it in the basic jig and routed the slots in it on my router table.

To attach the hinges accurately, I indexed both halves against the fixed rear fence, set a length of piano hinge in place, and used a small carpenter's square to align the hinges (see the top photo on p. 127). Then I drilled screw holes using the Vix bit and screwed the hinge on.

A small shopmade (turned) knob at the end of a carriage bolt secures the tenoning jig to a T-nut in the underside of the cross-cut box's base. The fixed rear fence ensures that the face of the tenoning jig stays parallel to the blade. Two brass lid supports hold a set angle securely (see the bottom photo on p. 127). And a hold-down clamp travels in a slot in the upper portion of the jig, allowing me to hold almost any size workpiece securely (see the photo at left, above).

Corner Slotting Jig

The corner slotting jig, which attaches directly to the tenoning jig, is easy to build and simple to use. I screwed two scrap boards to a backboard to form a 90° carriage positioned at 45° to the base of the crosscut box (see the drawing on p. 125). I cut a brace to fit up a few inches from the corner of the 90° carriage and across whatever it is I'm slotting. A hole through the backboard permits a hold-down clamp to bear on the brace, distributing the pressure of the clamp.

In use, I slide the workpiece into place and then the brace; then I tighten the clamp. The jig feels solid and works well.

KEN PICOU is a designer and woodworker in Austin, Texas.

Sliding Fence for a Miter Gauge

The piece of scrap I kept bolted to my tablesaw miter gauge was a great improvement over the gauge alone, especially when making crosscuts. This extra fence made the gauge easier to grip, and it supported the workpiece right up to the blade. The problem came when making angled cuts. Each new angle made a new divot in the fence, and pretty soon, it looked like an old comb with missing teeth. I would try to save time by using one of the gaps as a point of reference when cutting, but sooner or later, I'd use the wrong one. Then I'd get ticked off and have to stop work to make a new fence, and the whole cycle would start again.

I finally took the time to make a fence that could be moved right or left and locked in place by simply flipping two little levers (see the photo below). Now I can make minute adjustments in the position of a workpiece by releasing the levers and

BY TIM HANSON

THE LEVER-ACTION ADJUSTMENT on this shop-built fence lets you position the fence quickly.

The Sliding Miter Fence

Made from scrap lumber and easy-to-find hardware, this adjustable fence supports the work right up to the blade, no matter what the angle. It makes crosscutting and miter cutting safer and more efficient.

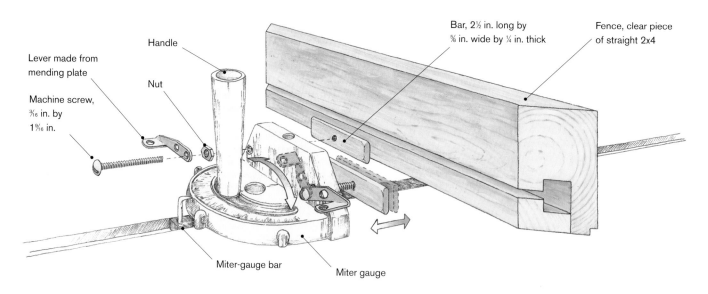

Lever made from mending plate

Handle

Machine screw, ³⁄₁₆ in. by 1⁹⁄₁₆ in.

Nut

Bar, 2½ in. long by ⅝ in. wide by ¼ in. thick

Fence, clear piece of straight 2x4

Miter-gauge bar

Miter gauge

THIS SLIDING FENCE IS EASY TO GRIP WITH HANDS OR CLAMPS. It also supports the work right up to the blade.

sliding the fence rather than unclamping and reclamping. The fence makes using the tablesaw faster, safer and more accurate.

How it Works

The wooden fence is held to the miter gauge by a pair of machine screws. The screws go through the miter gauge and are tapped into 2½-in.-long metal bars that ride in T-slots in the back of the fence. When the machine screws are loosened, the fence can be adjusted right or left—exactly where you want it. Flip the levers up, and the fence slides right up to the blade (see the photo at left). Flip them down, and the fence is locked in place.

The fence is made from a clear, straight piece of 2x4 construction lumber. I made it 20 in. long thinking I'd shorten it later, but I found the length useful when crosscutting long pieces.

I used a tablesaw to make the T-slot, but there are other ways to do it. The important thing is to make the slot larger than the bar stock by about ⅟₁₆ in. all around for easy sliding.

Fine-tuning the levers I fashioned the levers from right-angle mending plates, which I purchased at the hardware store. The drawings at right show the parts and how they go together, but the system does need some fine-tuning. Secure the levers under the heads of the machine screws with a wrench-tight nut. Slide the machine-screw assemblies through the miter gauge, and turn the bars onto the screws so the ends of the screws are flush with the bars.

Now turn one lever all the way to the left (at the 9 o'clock position), and slide the bar into the T-slot. Flip the lever to the right. The fence should tighten up against the miter gauge at about the 2 o'clock position without much effort. If it rotates past that point and the fence still isn't tight, the lever has to be repositioned. Disassemble the fence, and remove the machine screw. Clamp the machine screw between two blocks of wood in the vise, and loosen the nut just enough to rotate the lever counter-clockwise about one-quarter turn. Tighten the nut, and reassemble. It may take a few tries to get the levers to grip and release in the correct position. Use the same procedures to adjust the second bar.

Precise cuts come from an accurate fence. My miter gauge's face wasn't perpendicular to the table, so I had to handplane the wooden sliding fence to make it square.

TIM HANSON builds furniture and toys in Indianapolis, Ind.

Sliding Fence

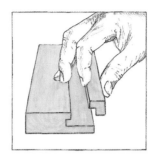

Make a T-shaped slot in the fence. Cut the pieces to the dimensions shown at right, and glue together. Make sure the bar stock moves freely in the slot. Miter the ends of the fence at 45°.

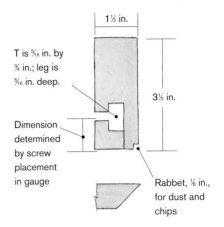

T is ⁵⁄₁₆ in. by ¾ in.; leg is ⁵⁄₁₆ in. deep.

1½ in.

3½ in.

Dimension determined by screw placement in gauge

Rabbet, ⅛ in., for dust and chips

Levers

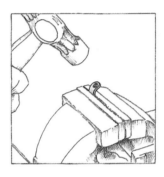

Make two levers from 2-in. by 2-in. mending plates. Cut one leg about ½ in. long, and round all the corners. Make the left lever by bending the short leg toward the back of the vise, as shown. For the right lever, bend the short leg toward the front.

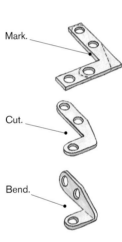

Mark.

Cut.

Bend.

Bars

A machine screw threads into the bar to lock the fence in position. If you don't have metal taps to make this connection, you can use a standard nut, as shown at right.

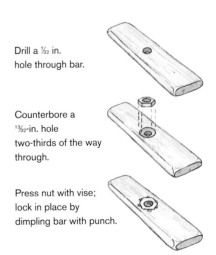

Drill a ⁷⁄₃₂ in. hole through bar.

Counterbore a ¹³⁄₃₂-in. hole two-thirds of the way through.

Press nut with vise; lock in place by dimpling bar with punch.

A Tablesaw Sled for Precision Crosscutting

BY LON SCHLEINING

Crosscutting with a standard tablesaw miter gauge can be frustrating, inaccurate, even hazardous. Adding an extended fence helps, but the miter gauge still will be limited and imprecise. Don't bother with it. Instead, take the time to make a super-accurate, super-versatile, and far safer crosscut sled.

A crosscut sled is a sliding table with runners that guide it over the saw in the miter-gauge slots. It has a rear fence set perpendicular to the line of cut to hold the workpiece. Because it uses both miter slots, the sled is remarkably and reliably accurate. It also easily accepts any number of stop blocks, auxiliary fences, and templates,

 MITERS.

CROSSCUTS.

TENONS.

allowing miters, tenons, and many other specialty cuts. Nearly every small commercial shop I know uses some variation of this sled. I use mine primarily to square the ends of 12-in.-wide stair treads.

Your sled should fit your work. There's no sense in making a huge, unwieldy sled if you'll use it mostly to cut 3-in. tenons. The one I use is 30 in. wide and 21 in. deep. It's capable of crosscutting a board up to 2 in. thick and 18 in. wide (see the photo on the facing page). With a miter template (see "From 90° to 45° Cuts with a Simple Template" on p. 136), the sled can cut a 45° miter on the end of a 3-in.-wide board. The rear fence is 5 in. high in the middle, 2½ in. high on the ends. Though I rarely crosscut a board thicker than 2 in., the fence needs to be at least 4 in. high to accommodate the height of the sawblade. The extra fence height also supports workpieces on end when I cut tenons.

Start with a Solid Platform of Baltic Birch Plywood

I build jigs like this from what I call not-yet-used materials (some call it scrap). I used void-free ½-in. Baltic birch plywood for the platform. Baltic birch is often mistaken for Finnish birch—its waterproof and much more costly cousin. Baltic birch is not as high quality, but for the price (about $1 per square foot), it's perfect for making

stable, durable jigs. But any plywood you have around the shop will probably work fine as long as it's flat.

The first step is to cut the platform to size. Make the platform as square as you can get it. You can check for square by measuring diagonally across the corners: The measurements should be the same across both corners. But before you make the sled, it's a good idea to make sure your tablesaw is tuned up.

For the sled to perform well, your saw's blade must be precisely parallel with the miter-gauge slots, and the table must be flat.

Quartersawn Hardwood Runners for Smooth Sliding

I prefer to make runners from oak, instead of buying steel ones, because I can control their fit in the miter slots. Wood runners pose a few problems, however, that should be taken into consideration. Expansion from seasonal humidity can cause them to bind in the miter slots, so I choose the material and its grain orientation carefully. They also need to be milled precisely.

Start with a close-grained flatsawn maple or oak board. Mill the thickness of the board to the width of the slot using a planer. Test the fit as you go, planing off a little material at a time. It should slide easily in the slot, but without slop (see the photos

T ailor the size of the sled to fit the work you do. The crucial features are a rear fence perpendicular to the line of cut and runners that slide easily without slop.

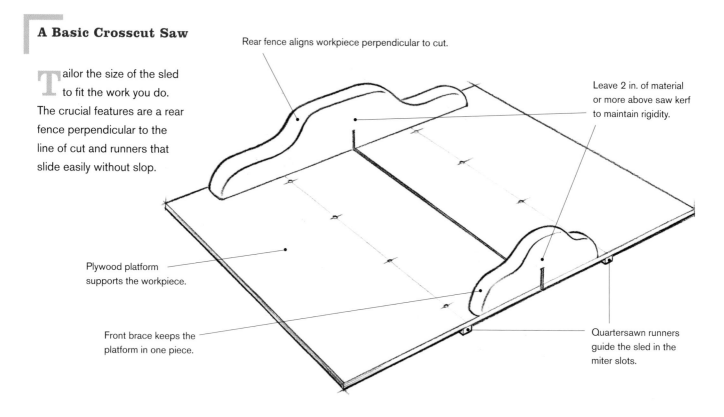

Rear fence aligns workpiece perpendicular to cut.

Leave 2 in. of material or more above saw kerf to maintain rigidity.

Plywood platform supports the workpiece.

Front brace keeps the platform in one piece.

Quartersawn runners guide the sled in the miter slots.

on the facing page). Next, rip two runners from the board to a thickness slightly less than the depth of the miter slots, then cut them to length. By ripping strips off a flat-grained board, you have made quartersawn runners, which will be very stable. The idea is to make runners that don't rub against the bottom of the slots and raise the sled off the table, but that still engage as much of the miter slot as possible.

The first construction step is to fasten the runners to the platform. To make sure they are right where they should be, attach them while they're in the miter slots. Lower the blade out of the way, and center the platform on the table, using the rip fence to keep the platform square on the runners (see the left photo on the facing page). Lay out the holes for the screws so they're centered on the runners, and drill them in the platform only. The screws should pass freely through the holes in the plywood.

The size of the drill bit you choose for the pilot holes in the runners is very important. Thin runners will bulge or split if the pilot hole is too small. Even a small bulge

will make the runner bind in the miter slot. The holes should be slightly larger than the shank diameter of the screw. I use a dial caliper to measure the shank, and then I select the correct drill bit. On this sled, I used ⅝-in.-long #8 screws that have a shank diameter of 0.122 in., so a ⅛-in. drill bit (0.125 in.) was perfect.

First drill just one pilot hole in each runner, and insert a screw in each. These screws keep the runners firmly in place while you drill the other pilot holes. Remove the two screws, deburr all the holes, apply a small bead of glue to the runners and screw the platform to the runners. Clean off any glue that might have squeezed out.

Now take your incomplete sled for a test drive: move it back and forth in the miter slots to see if it runs smoothly. It's easy to tell just where the oak runners are binding because they'll be shiny and gray from rubbing against the sides of the steel slots. While the glue is still soft, it is possible to move the runners slightly. You only should be concerned at this point with how smoothly the platform slides.

Make Front Brace and Rear Fence

The front brace's only job is to keep the platform in one piece. It doesn't much matter what size or shape it is (I add some gentle curves to mine) as long as it is a few inches higher than the sawblade's maximum cut—about 2 in. above the platform. I made this brace from 1¼-in.-thick red oak, 3¾ in. high, and about as long as the width between the miter slots. Shape it, smooth it, and glue and screw it to the front of the table from the underside of the platform.

This is also the time to make the rear fence. I used some 2-in.-thick white oak 5 in. wide and 23 in. long. The rear fence should be pretty stout to hold the sled table together. If you don't have 8/4 lumber, laminate two 4/4 pieces together. Make sure the board is perfectly straight on the inside face and square with the edge that will be attached to the platform.

Keeping things square becomes critical when you attach the rear fence. The most important thing to remember when making a sled is that, for the cut to be square, the rear fence must be square to the line of cut. If it's not, you have a useless sled.

Before you attach the rear fence, put the sled on the saw, raise the blade slightly above the thickness of the platform and cut through the platform about two-thirds of the way from back to front, being very careful not to cut all the way through the platform (see the photos on p. 137). Drill and countersink the holes in the platform, then securely clamp the fence to the platform so that it is square to the cut you just made. Use an accurate framing square to align it, checking from both sides of the fence. Now drill two center pilot holes

Start with the Runners

A PERFECT FIT. Runner stock should slide freely in the miter slots (left). Finished runners should be just below the level of the table (right).

Attach the Platform to the Runners

USE MITER SLOTS TO ALIGN RUNNERS UNDER PLATFORM. The rip fence keeps the platform square and centered while you lay out (left) and drill the pilot holes (right). To avoid splitting the runners, the holes should be slightly larger than the shank diameter of the screw.

From 90° to 45° Cuts with a Simple Template

With this template, you'll be able to make accurate miter cuts on your tablesaw. The template is nothing more than a piece of Baltic birch plywood with two sides at 90° to each other and a back side that registers against the rear fence of the sled. This template sits far enough forward so that long workpieces clear the ends of the rear fence.

There are any number of ways to make such a shape. I used the opportunity to test the accuracy of my sled. First I laid out and rough cut the template from a corner of a sheet of plywood and got one of the sides straight on a jointer. This

can also be done on the sled by aligning the edge over the saw kerf and nailing the template to the sled (don't let the nails go all the way through). I then cut the opposite side at 90° to the first using the rear fence.

To cut the base at 45° to the two sides, I cut to the layout line on the base by aligning it over the kerf and nailing the template to the sled. I've rarely gotten a base perfect the first time.

To find out which way it's out, I center the point of the template on the saw kerf and align the base against the rear fence. Then I scribe its outline on the sled. I flip it over

and check it against the scribe marks. If it sits perfectly between the lines, I'm on the money.

If not, I recut the back of the template as required. Finally, I attach it to the sled with a few screws, make some trial miters and adjust accordingly.

(of four total) into the fence, and install the screws from the bottom side.

Before you can attach the rear fence once and for all, make some trial crosscuts, and check the results. The position of the fence will almost certainly need fine-tuning. It's easy to rotate the rear fence back and forth a little with hammer taps or a bar clamp, even with the two screws snug. This is where patience is important. Keep making test cuts and adjusting as necessary until the cut is perfectly square. Don't, however, cut all the way through the platform at this time. Leave just enough plywood at the rear of the platform to hold the sled together; if you cut all the way through, the rear fence will be harder to align.

Attach the Rear Fence, and Make More Trial Cuts

When the sled makes true 90° crosscuts, it's time to attach the rear fence permanently. Clamp a long 4-in. by 4-in. block to the sled platform so that it fits tight against the rear fence. It will keep the fence's place. Remove the two screws that are temporarily holding the fence. Apply glue, and reinstall the fence with the rest of the screws. Carefully check its position against the block. Remove the clamps and the block, and immediately make a trial cut, still without cutting all the way through the platform.

Adjust the fence if necessary with hammer taps or clamps. Even though the sled is screwed and glued together at this point, it's still possible to make fine adjustments, but only for a few minutes after glue-up.

Before you spend too much time admiring your handy work, sand all the sharp edges, and coat the bottom with a lubricant such as spray silicone or TopCote®. Even then, you're not done. You still have guide blocks and templates to make. They will let your sled cut perfect tenons and miters.

LON SCHLEINING is a woodworker in Dana Point, Calif. He is the author of *Treasure Chests* (2001) and *The Workbench* (2004), both by The Taunton Press, Inc.

Use the Kerf to Square the Fence

DON'T CUT THAT SLED IN HALF. After you attach the front brace (left), cut only two-thirds of the way through the platform (right). The kerf is a reference to set the rear fence.

SQUARE THE FENCE TO THE SAW KERF. Check the fence's alignment from both sides of the kerf. Attach the fence with only two screws before you make trial cuts.

Shopmade Rip Fence Assembles Easily, Stays Aligned

BY WORTH BARTON

When I bought an older-model 10-in. Craftsman tablesaw, I was pleased with the saw's operation, but I was frustrated by its rip fence. It was a pitifully thin zinc die-casted saddle that soon broke. I could have bought one of the many after-market rip fences that are available. But I knew that I could make a sturdy, accurate rip fence fairly inexpensively (mine cost about $65*) following a few simple ideas (see the photos on p. 140).

Design

Building a first-rate replacement rip fence is pure fun—good for the shop and for the ego. I began by making a "got to have" list:

- Strength, durability and deflection resistance
- Reasonably available components
- Construction requiring only a drill press and hand tools
- Repeatable settings with low-friction movement
- Consistent clamping behavior
- Quick removal

Using square tube steel for the fence took care of the first three items, and a toggle clamp in the saddle satisfied the last three.

Steel parts plus single-rail locking equal precision Most impressive of the commercial rip fences are the cast-iron and steel ones that marry precise surfaces to smooth movement. I decided to capitalize on those principles using common steel sections bolted together. I also decided to use a single-rail locking mechanism. Here's why: Many commercial rip fences, once positioned, get locked to both the front and rear guide rails. But when I checked a couple of fences of this type using a dial indicator, I found that the locking action would slightly skew the fence out of parallel. So on my rip fence, I made a saddle that has a toggle-clamp plunger offset below two guide bolts at the front rail (see the drawing detail on the facing page). This provides the fence with the necessary down pressure (to the table), which means that I don't need a clip at the rear rail. Though the rip fence still requires a rear rail, it is for guidance only—not for latching the rip fence in position.

The saddle. The piece that connects the fence to the front guide rail, the saddle, is really the key. I chose a long base for the saddle to control what aircraft and boat designers call pitch, roll, and yaw. To picture these phenomena, think of the fence as an airplane's fuselage. Pitch refers to the degree of nose-to-tail level. Roll is side-to-side

Rip Fence Construction

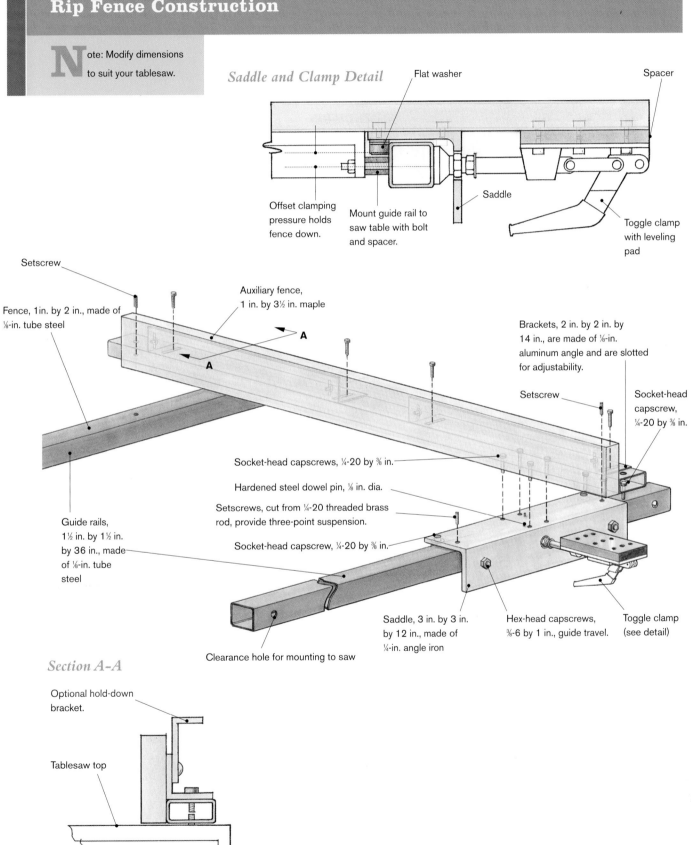

Note: Modify dimensions to suit your tablesaw.

Saddle and Clamp Detail

Flat washer

Spacer

Offset clamping pressure holds fence down.

Mount guide rail to saw table with bolt and spacer.

Saddle

Toggle clamp with leveling pad

Setscrew

Fence, 1 in. by 2 in., made of ⅛-in. tube steel

Auxiliary fence, 1 in. by 3½ in. maple

A

A

Brackets, 2 in. by 2 in. by 14 in., are made of ⅛-in. aluminum angle and are slotted for adjustability.

Setscrew

Socket-head capscrew, ¼-20 by ⅜ in.

Socket-head capscrews, ¼-20 by ⅜ in.

Hardened steel dowel pin, ⅛ in. dia.

Setscrews, cut from ¼-20 threaded brass rod, provide three-point suspension.

Socket-head capscrew, ¼-20 by ⅜ in.

Guide rails, 1½ in. by 1½ in. by 36 in., made of ⅛-in. tube steel

Saddle, 3 in. by 3 in. by 12 in., made of ¼-in. angle iron

Hex-head capscrews, ⅜-6 by 1 in., guide travel.

Toggle clamp (see detail)

Clearance hole for mounting to saw

Section A-A

Optional hold-down bracket.

Tablesaw top

RIP FENCE SLIDES SMOOTHLY, LOCKS POSITIVELY. Barton, setting up for a rip cut, snugs his fence in position using the saddle's toggle clamp. The fence, which has a hardwood auxiliary fence, was made out of standard steel sections and hardware. The fence slides on three brass setscrews that contact two square-tube guide rails.

THE UNDERSIDE OF THE SADDLE REVEALS HOW THE FENCE STAYS ALIGNED. Two socket-head screws (left side of angle) and a toggle clamp (right side of angle) sandwich the front guide rail. The saddle is fixed squarely to the fence by bolts and steel dowel pins. The two other bolts (with nuts) guide the fence during positioning.

(port to starboard) level. On the saw, these motions are relative to the table, the horizontal reference plane. To understand yaw, think of the fence's saddle as the tail of the airplane. The tail can swivel back and forth while remaining level with respect to the fuselage, as though the airplane were pivoting about a vertical axis. Yaw is similar on the saw, though it is greatly diminished; the rip fence can twist from side to side in the plane of the saw table, like a washing machine agitator.

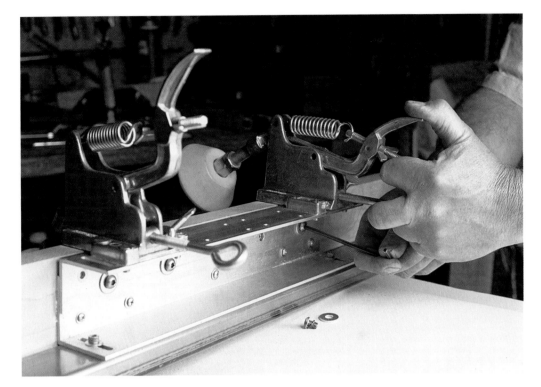

To control yaw when the saddle position is fixed, I mounted two guide bolts
(behind the front guide rail) and an
adjustable De-Sta-Co® toggle clamp
between the two bolts (ahead of the front
guide rail). The front rail is sandwiched
between the ball-and-socket pad on the
end of the clamp's plunger and the heads
of the screws. That keeps the fence perpendicular to the rail. Because the screws in the
saddle are above the plunger, clamping
pressure forces the fence onto the saw table.
This pressure enables the rip fence to resist
the uplift action of a hold-down device. I
use Shophelper hold-downs, available from
Woodworker's Supply℠, (see "Sources" on
p. 142), which have anti-kickback rollers.
Two additional bolts, widely spaced and
adjustable (see the bottom photo on the
facing page), control yaw when I slide the
saddle. This allows the motion to be smooth
and free from lock-up.

**Contact points: setscrews and guide
rails** To restrict pitch and roll, I made the
fence so it contacts the guide rails at three
places: Two saddle points ride on the front
rail (see the top photo on the facing page),

and one point on the end of the fence rides
along the rear rail. For the contact points, I
installed three brass setscrews, which provide a means of leveling and act as low-
friction bearings.

The guide rails must be square or rectangular because the saddle has to lock
positively to the front guide rail, and the
setscrews must slide on flat surfaces at both
the front and rear guide rails. If your tablesaw has pipe rails or angle-iron rails, replace
them with square-tube sections (see the
drawing on p. 139). To attach the rails, drill
through the flange (edge) of your saw table,
so you can use bolts and spacers to hold the
rails perpendicular to the miter slots and
parallel to the table surface. Set the rails
lower than the table, so the rails don't
interfere with the miter slots.

Materials, Fasteners, and Assembly

Because steel has three times the stiffness of
aluminum, I used standard structural steel
box shapes for the long members (the two
guide rails and the fence). The tube steel is
dimensionally uniform, has a high resistance

Sources

CLAMPS

(Note: modify thread to ⅜-16 for stud-type plunger pad.)

De-Sta-Co
PO Box 2800
250 Park St.
Troy, MI 48007
Phone: (313) 589-2008.
Web: www.
destacomanufacturing.com

ALUMINUM AND STEEL
Adjustable Clamp Co.
417 N. Ashland Ave.
Chicago, IL 60622;
Phone: (312) 666-2723
Web: www.adjustableclamp.com

Castle Metals
3400 N. Wolf Rd.
Franklin Park, IL 60131

Phone: (708) 455-7111
Web: www.amcastle.com

TOOLING ACCESSORIES AND FASTENERS
Reid Tool Supply Co.
2265 Black Creek Rd.
Muskegon, MI 49444-2684
Phone: (800) 253-0421
Web: www.reidtool.com

Vlier Corporation
2333 Valley St.
Burbank, CA 91505
Phone: (818) 843-1922
Web: www.vlier.com

SHOPHELPER HOLD-DOWNS
Woodworker's Supply
1108 N. Glenn Rd.
Casper, WY 82601
Phone: (505) 797-1487
Web: www.woodworker.com

capscrews are ideal because they are made of high-quality steel and install easily.

The saddle-fence assembly is essentially a T-square, which glides on the front and rear rails. A .005-in. to .015-in. gap between the table and the fence allows clearance for sawdust and promotes smooth movement. As a safety feature, I extended the fence over the toggle clamp (see the top photo on p. 140), which prevents me from accidentally bumping the actuating lever.

Slotted brackets attach the auxiliary fence to the main fence (see the photo on p. 141). A similar bracket attaches the optional hold-down. The main brackets are symmetrical so that the auxiliary fence can be placed right or left of the fence. The slots, unlike holes, allow the fence to be adjustable and skewed for 2° or 3° tapers. It also enables the fence to be opened slightly at the rear of the saw (mine skews .020 in. over its length), as opposed to being parallel to the blade. A flared rip fence lessens the likelihood of kickback when you're ripping wet or unstable wood.

Setup for Use

Make sure your sawblade and miter slots are parallel. Then set the fence parallel to the slots. To do this, place the assembly on the saw and attach a dial indicator to a miter-slot guide. Run the guide back and forth in the slot as you check the fence for runout. Tighten the screws joining the saddle to the fence. To ensure that the fence-saddle squareness won't be lost through rough handling, match-drill the parts so that you can press-fit hardened-steel dowel pins to lock the assembly: First clamp the saddle and fence together, and then drill and ream them to receive the pins. You can press in the pins with a drill press or tap them in with a hammer.

★Please note price estimates are from 1994.

WORTH BARTON is a design engineer, inventor and hobbyist woodworker living in San Jose, Calif.

to twisting, and is readily available at most metal-supply houses (see "Sources" above). I used ⅛-in.-thick wall tubing to avoid bolt tear-out in the tapped holes. Have your steel vendor cut the tubes to the exact length you need. For the saddle, I used a 12-in. length of ¼-in. by 3-in. by-3-in. angle iron. A model #607 De-Sta-Co toggle clamp locks the saddle; a piece of straight maple, attached by aluminum angles, serves as an auxiliary fence (see the drawing on p. 139).

I bolted the parts together rather than welding them. Struggling with welding distortion can ruin your day. By contrast, bolts are easy to drill and tap for and are easy to remove. Suppliers offer a wondrous variety of fastening and clamping devices (see "Sources"). I use short fasteners because they reduce connection springiness and still afford some adjustability. Socket-head

Shop-Built Extension Tables

BY DWAYNE J. INTVELD

When using a tablesaw to cut a large workpiece or a full sheet of plywood, it's important to provide extra support surfaces for the stock. But like many woodworkers, I don't have enough room in my shop to have extension tables permanently fixed in place. So after I recently added a new fence system to expand the ripping capacity of my tablesaw, I built a side table that readily folds down out of the way when not needed. This foldable table allows easy access to my grinding wheel, which is located adjacent to the tablesaw.

And while I was at it, I replaced my somewhat flimsy portable outfeed roller with a sturdy outfeed table that folds down behind the saw. I have the option of opening it in two stages, depending on my needs at the time. The first stage provides a 36-in. main outfeed table; the next stage produces a secondary outfeed table that adds about another 30 in. to the main table, handy for extralong stock.

Although the side and outfeed tables enhance the versatility of my tablesaw, the impact on shop space has been minimal. With both tables open, a 4x8 sheet of plywood remains supported throughout the entire cut. Yet, when folded, the tables add little to the footprint of the saw.

A Few Caveats to Consider

Remember that the drawing dimensions are based on building the tables to fit my 10-in. Powermatic 66 tablesaw, which sits on a 2-in.-tall wood frame. The extra couple of inches raises the top of the table to

36 in., a height better suited to my 6-ft., 4-in. frame.

Also, the rip-fence system on my table-saw is made by Biesemeyer®. If you use a different type, unless it's a Biesemeyer clone, you'll likely need to modify the way the tables connect to the saw, especially at the outfeed end.

Finally, because the outfeed table sits just behind the saw when folded up, the table won't work with a saw that has a motor or any other obstruction sticking out the back. The side table, however, should be adapt-able to any saw.

Side Table

The side table consists of a tabletop, a con-nector that joins the tabletop to the saw and a side leg frame that supports the table-top when it's open.

The table and the connector are made of a maple frame rabbeted to accept ¾-in.-thick particleboard. To create a smoother surface with extra durability, I added plastic laminate to the top face.

To make the leg frame, I cut grooves in 1¼-in.-thick maple rails and stiles to accept a ¼-in.-thick maple plywood panel. For added strength, I glued the panel into the grooves.

Once the leg frame was assembled, I joined it to the outboard end of the table-top with a piano hinge. When folded, the leg frame ends up neatly housed in the tabletop frame, held in place by a pair of double-ball catches.

Although not shown here, I added a 1½-in. square leg between my shop floor and the right end of the Biesemeyer front rail. The leg provides additional support for the rail when the side table is opened. To allow for length adjustment of the leg, I installed a threaded insert in the bottom end of the leg, then I added a carriage bolt with a locking nut into the insert. The length of the leg can be fine-tuned to an uneven floor simply by threading the carriage bolt in or out.

Outfeed Table

I built the main and secondary outfeed tables using torsion-box construction, a technique that sandwiches strips of grid-work between thin outer skins. The resulting structure is strong and stiff—much like a honeycomb—yet it's relatively lightweight.

First I made the four-sided maple frames of the torsion boxes, then I glued one of the ¼-in.-thick medium-density fiberboard (MDF) skins to each frame. I then filled these shallow boxes with strips of ¾-in. by ¾-in. pine, half-lapped and glued to the MDF. On the main tabletop, the grid includes two wider strips. These wide strips align with the two miter-gauge slots on the tablesaw when the tabletop is mounted to the saw. The wider stock allowed me to rout a pair of grooves in the top to provide clearance for the miter-gauge bar.

Once the gridwork was in place, I was ready to add the second skin to the top of the boxes. First, a coat of glue was applied to all box and gridwork surfaces that would

THE TABLES ALMOST DISAP-
PEAR. **Shop space grows considerably when the extension
tables fold down.**

mate with the skin. I put the skin on top, then added a few bricks, which provided all the clamping pressure I needed. After that, I applied plastic laminate to both faces of each tabletop.

Outfeed leg frame adds support The outfeed leg frame is made up of a single rail mortised into a pair of stiles. A piano hinge serves as the remaining side of the frame, and it provides a means to mount the leg frame to the main outfeed table.

The secondary outfeed table nests inside the leg frame, mounted to the same hinge. But to allow the top to pivot independently of the leg frame, I cut one leaf of the hinge in two places, with the cuts made just inside the edges of the stiles. By the way, two ½-in. rabbets—one on the rail and one on the secondary table—work together to create a simple stop.

A pair of drawbolts keeps the leg frame and secondary table together as a single unit while swinging to an opened or closed position. I couldn't find drawbolts that suited my needs, so I ended up making my own.

Fill gap with a spacer The outfeed table is supported by the rear rail of the Biesemeyer

fence. I shortened the rear rail's length to 45 in. so that it attached only to the table of the saw and the connector piece for the side table. Also, I enlarged the holes used to mount the rail to the saw. The larger holes gave me wiggle room to fine-tune the height of the table.

A spacer, made from maple, was added to the rear rail to elevate the outfeed table so that it ends up flush with the saw table. The lengthwise rabbet in the spacer provides clearance for the bolts that secure the rail to the saw. To attach the spacer, I bored $\frac{3}{16}$-in.-diameter holes, spaced 8 in. apart, through the rail. Then I screwed the spacer to the rail with #12 roundhead wood screws.

At this point, I applied varnish to all exposed maple surfaces. Then I adjusted the carriage-bolt feet to get everything level. After that, and probably for the first time ever, I actually looked forward to cutting a full sheet of plywood.

DWAYNE J. INTVELD is an engineering manager living in Hazel Green, Wisc.

Side Table

How the Tables Are Attached

Side Table

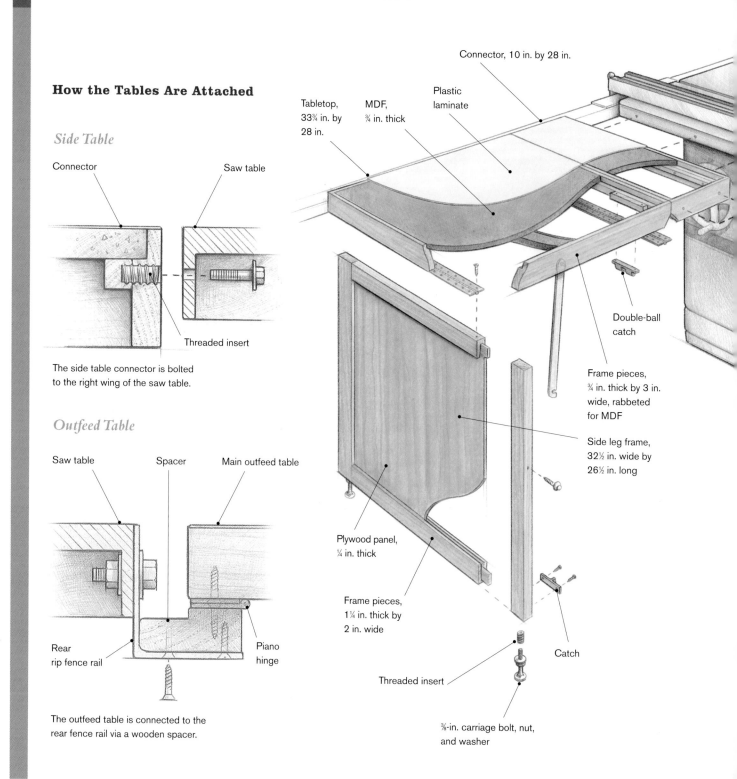

Connector

Saw table

Threaded insert

The side table connector is bolted to the right wing of the saw table.

Outfeed Table

Saw table

Spacer

Main outfeed table

Rear rip fence rail

Piano hinge

The outfeed table is connected to the rear fence rail via a wooden spacer.

Connector, 10 in. by 28 in.

Tabletop, 33¾ in. by 28 in.

MDF, ¾ in. thick

Plastic laminate

Double-ball catch

Frame pieces, ¾ in. thick by 3 in. wide, rabbeted for MDF

Side leg frame, 32½ in. wide by 26½ in. long

Plywood panel, ¼ in. thick

Frame pieces, 1¼ in. thick by 2 in. wide

Catch

Threaded insert

⅜-in. carriage bolt, nut, and washer

Outfeed Table

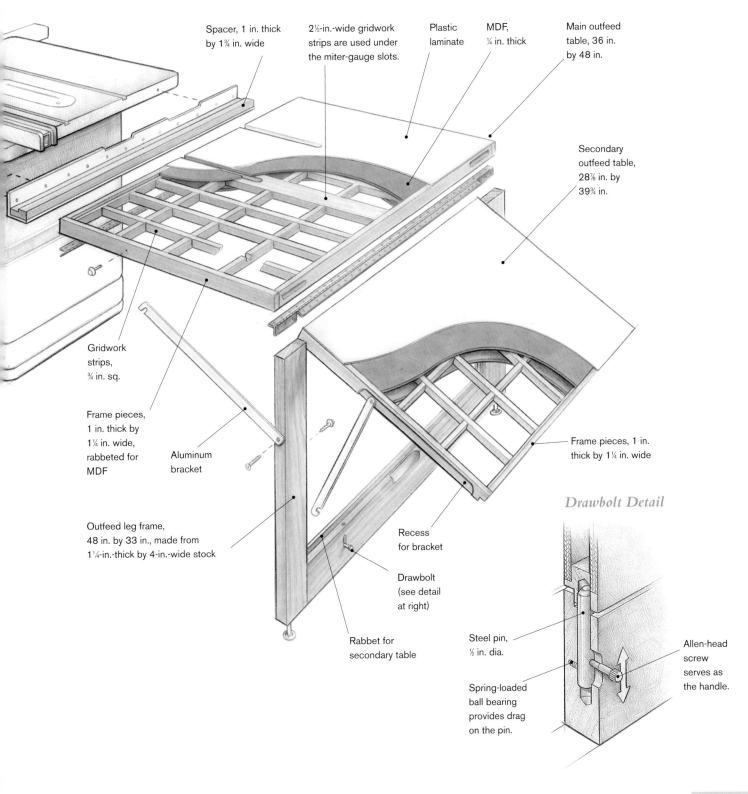

Spacer, 1 in. thick by 1¾ in. wide

2½-in.-wide gridwork strips are used under the miter-gauge slots.

Plastic laminate

MDF, ¼ in. thick

Main outfeed table, 36 in. by 48 in.

Secondary outfeed table, 28⅞ in. by 39¾ in.

Gridwork strips, ¾ in. sq.

Frame pieces, 1 in. thick by 1¼ in. wide, rabbeted for MDF

Aluminum bracket

Outfeed leg frame, 48 in. by 33 in., made from 1¼-in.-thick by 4-in.-wide stock

Rabbet for secondary table

Recess for bracket

Drawbolt (see detail at right)

Frame pieces, 1 in. thick by 1¼ in. wide

Drawbolt Detail

Steel pin, ½ in. dia.

Spring-loaded ball bearing provides drag on the pin.

Allen-head screw serves as the handle.

Credits

The articles in this book appeared in the following issues of *Fine Woodworking*:

p. 4: Nine Midsize Tablesaws by Roland Johnson, issue 167. Photos by William Duckworth, courtesy *Fine Woodworking*, © The Taunton Press, Inc.

p. 14: Ten-Inch Combination Tablesaw Blades by Tom Begnal, issue 155. Photos by Michael Pekovich, courtesy *Fine Woodworking*, © The Taunton Press, Inc. except photos on pp. 15, 16 (left) and 18 (bottom left) by Erika Marks, courtesy *Fine Woodworking*, © The Taunton Press, Inc.

p. 22: A Tablesaw Primer: Ripping and Crosscutting by Kelly Mehler, issue 167. Drawings by Jim Richey, courtesy *Fine Woodworking*, © The Taunton Press, Inc.

p. 31: Joint-Quality Edges Cut on a Tablesaw by Lon Schleining, issue 129. Photos by Strother Purdy, courtesy *Fine Woodworking*, © The Taunton Press, Inc. except photo on p. 36 by Joe Romeo, © The Taunton Press, Inc.

p. 37: Safe Procedures at the Tablesaw by Howard Lewin, issue 132. Photos and drawings by Michael Pekovich, courtesy *Fine Woodworking*, © The Taunton Press, Inc.

p. 45: Taming Tearout on the Tablesaw by Steve Latta, issue 168. Photos by Matt Berger, courtesy *Fine Woodworking*, © The Taunton Press, Inc.; Drawings by Kelly J. Dutton, courtesy *Fine Woodworking*, © The Taunton Press, Inc.

p. 50: Cutting Coves on the Tablesaw by Stuart Sabol, issue 166.

Photos by Mark Schofield, courtesy *Fine Woodworking*, © The Taunton Press, Inc.; Drawings by Vince Babak, courtesy *Fine Woodworking*, © The Taunton Press, Inc.

p. 59: Pattern Cutting on the Tablesaw by Steve Latta, issue 155. Photos by Anatole Burkin, courtesy *Fine Woodworking*, © The Taunton Press, Inc.; Drawings by Jim Richey, courtesy *Fine Woodworking*, © The Taunton Press, Inc.

p. 64: Box Joints on the Tablesaw by Lon Schleining, issue 168. Photos by Matthew Teague, courtesy *Fine Woodworking*, © The Taunton Press, Inc.; Drawings by Vince Babak, courtesy *Fine Woodworking*, © The Taunton Press, Inc.

p. 70: Tablesawn Dovetails by Steve Latta, issue 152. Photos by Asa Christiana, courtesy *Fine Woodworking*, © The Taunton Press, Inc.; Drawings by Kelly J. Dutton, courtesy *Fine Woodworking*, © The Taunton Press, Inc.

p. 78: Machine Dovetails by Eye by Jeff Miller, issue 120. Photos by Aimé Fraser, courtesy *Fine Woodworking*, © The Taunton Press, Inc.; Drawings by Vince Babak, courtesy *Fine Woodworking*, © The Taunton Press, Inc.

p. 83: Shopmade Tenoning Jig by Brad Schilling, issue 154. Photos by Tom Begnal, courtesy *Fine Woodworking*, © The Taunton Press, Inc.; Drawings by Jim Richey, courtesy *Fine Woodworking*, © The Taunton Press, Inc.

p. 88: Angled Tenons on the Tablesaw by William Krase, issue 99. Photos by Vincent Laurence, courtesy *Fine Woodworking*, © The Taunton Press, Inc.

p. 90: Joinery for Curved Work by Garrett Hack, issue 137. Photos by Anatole Burkin, courtesy *Fine Woodworking*, © The Taunton Press, Inc.; Drawings by Michael Pekovich, courtesy *Fine Woodworking*, © The Taunton Press, Inc.

p. 96: Dust-Proof Your Contractor's Saw by Dick McDonough, issue 145. Photos by Michael Pekovich, courtesy *Fine Woodworking*, © The Taunton Press, Inc. except photo on p. 96 by Tom Begnal; Drawings by Vince Babak, courtesy *Fine Woodworking*, © The Taunton Press, Inc.

p. 102: Shopmade Tablesaw Guards by Sandor Nagyszalanczy, issue 104. Photos by Sandor Nagyszalanczy, courtesy *Fine Woodworking*, © The Taunton Press, Inc.

p. 108: Causes and Prevention of Tablesaw Kickback by Kelly Mehler, issue 116. Photos by Dennis Preston, courtesy *Fine Woodworking*, © The Taunton Press, Inc. except photo on p. 108 by Boyd Hagen, courtesy *Fine Woodworking*, © The Taunton Press, Inc.; Drawings by Jim Richey, courtesy *Fine Woodworking*, © The Taunton Press, Inc.

p. 113: Tablesaw Kickback by Lon Schleining, issue 139. Photos by Joe Romeo except photo on p. 113 by Matthew Teague; courtesy *Fine Woodworking*, © The Taunton Press, Inc.; Drawings by Vince Babak, courtesy *Fine Woodworking*, © The Taunton Press, Inc.

p. 118: Reproducing Your Project by Ken Picou, issue 104. Photos by Vincent Laurence, courtesy *Fine Woodworking*, © The Taunton Press, Inc.

p. 120: Making a Sliding Saw Table by Guy Perez, issue 101. Photos by Alec Waters, courtesy *Fine Woodworking*, © The Taunton Press, Inc.; Drawings by David Dann.

p. 124: One-Stop Cutting Station by Ken Picou, issue 107. Photos by Vincent Laurence, courtesy *Fine Woodworking*, © The Taunton Press, Inc.; Drawings by Michael Gellatly, courtesy *Fine Woodworking*, © The Taunton Press, Inc.

p. 129: Sliding Fence for a Miter Gauge by Tim Hanson, issue 118. Photos by Aimé Fraser, courtesy *Fine Woodworking*, © The Taunton Press, Inc.; Drawings by Christopher Clapp, courtesy *Fine Woodworking*, © The Taunton Press, Inc.

p. 132: A Tablesaw Sled for Pecision Crosscutting by Lon Schleining, issue 128. Photos by Strother Purdy, courtesy *Fine Woodworking*, © The Taunton Press, Inc.; Drawings by Michael Pekovich, courtesy *Fine Woodworking*, © The Taunton Press, Inc.

p. 138: Shopmade Rip Fence Assembles Easily, Stays Aligned by Worth Barton, issue 109. Photos by Alec Waters, courtesy *Fine Woodworking*, © The Taunton Press, Inc.; Drawings by Kathleen Rushton, courtesy *Fine Woodworking*, © The Taunton Press, Inc.

p. 143: Shop-Built Extension Tables by Dwayne J. Intveld, issue 163. Photos by Tom Begnal, courtesy *Fine Woodworking*, © The Taunton Press, Inc.; Drawings by Bob La Pointe, courtesy *Fine Woodworking*, © The Taunton Press, Inc.

Index